THE IMITATION
OF CHRIST

The Imitation of Christ

by

Thomas à Kempis

Translated from the original Latin by the Right Rev.
Richard Challoner, D.D.

Baronius Press
MMVIII

First published in 2006 by
BARONIUS PRESS LTD
London · United Kingdom · www.baroniuspress.com

© Baronius Press Limited, 2006.
This edition 2008.

10 9 8 7 6 5 4 3 2

ISBN (13 digit): 978-1-905574-06-3

This edition has been re-typeset using the text of the 1893 edition originally published by Desclée, Lefebbre & Co., Belgium, with an Imprimatur by G. F. J. Bouvry Vic. Gen., Tournai, 28th September 1893.

Cover Picture: An artist's impression of the Christ Child from *The Madonna delle Ombre* by Fra Angelico.

Printed in India.

CONTENTS

BOOK II
Admonitions Concerning Interior Things

BOOK III
Of Internal Consolation

BOOK IV
Of the Blessed Sacrament

PREFACE

The Imitation of Christ is the most famous devotional book ever written. Indeed, it is second only to the Bible as the most popular Christian book in existence. It has been an integral part of the spiritual reading of the saints ever since it first appeared anonymously in 1418. It is not uncommon to read of saints whose whole library consisted of the Bible, the liturgical books and the *Imitation*; and its popularity extends even to the Protestant world. The author of this remarkable work, Thomas à Kempis, was born in Kempen, in the Diocese of Cologne, in 1379 or 1380. In 1399, he joined the Canons Regular of Windesheim, where he remained until his death in 1471, twice being elected subprior.

The Canons Regular of Windesheim were among the leaders of the reforming movement in Northern Europe at this time. It was the period of declining mediaeval unity, which nonetheless produced many of the works we think of as most characteristically mediaeval – the *Divine Comedy*, the *Dialogue* of St. Catherine of Sienna and the writings of the Rhineland mystics. The Canons of Windesheim were concerned not only with the improvement of morals among the clergy, but also with extending and deepening the spiritual life of the laity in the promotion of the *Devotio Moderna*, a form of spirituality which finds its finest expression in *The Imitation of Christ*.

As Christopher Dawson has observed, the spirituality of this period "concentrated its attention on the Humanity of Jesus, on the contemplation of his Life and Passion, and on the practice of the Imitation of Christ. These are the characteristic notes of mediaeval devotion, from the time of the reforming movement, down to the Protestant Reformation, from St. Anselm and St. Bernard to St. Francis and St. Bonaventure, down to the Yorkshire hermit Richard Rolle and Thomas à Kempis." We might mention as particular influences to be found in the Imitation: the Sacred Scriptures, St. Augustine, St. Bernard, and the school of Windesheim.

But these are technicalities – of interest to the scholar, but apt to be misleading to the general reader: for the *Imitation* is a masterwork with a flavour very much its own, and cannot readily be mistaken for any other book. It is presented here in its best known English translation: that of the Venerable Richard Challoner (1691 - 1781), Vicar Apostolic of the London district in penal times, and perhaps the greatest English Catholic figure of the eighteenth century.

Robert Asch

BOOK I

Useful Admonitions for a Spiritual Life

CHAPTER I
Following Christ

"HE that followeth me, walketh not in darkness," saith Our Lord. (John 8:12). These are the words of Christ, by which we are admonished, that we must imitate His life and manners, if we would be truly enlightened, and delivered from all blindness of heart.

Let it then be our chief study to meditate on the life of Jesus Christ.

2. The doctrine of Christ surpasseth all the doctrines of the saints, and whosoever hath the spirit will find therein a hidden manna. (Apoc. 2:17).

But it happeneth that many, by frequent hearing of the Gospel, are very little affected: because they have not the spirit of Christ.

But he who would fully and feelingly understand the words of Christ, must study to make his whole life conformable to that of Christ.

3. What doth it avail thee to discourse profoundly of the Trinity if thou be void of humility, and consequently, displeasing to the Trinity?

In truth, sublime words make not a man holy and just: but a virtuous life maketh him dear to God.

I would rather feel compunction, than know its definition.

If thou didst know the whole Bible by heart, and the sayings of all the philosophers, what would it all profit thee without the love of God and His grace?

"Vanity of vanities, and all is vanity" (Eccles. 1:2), besides loving God and serving Him alone.

This is the highest wisdom, by despising the world to tend to heavenly kingdoms.

4. It is vanity, therefore, to seek after riches which must perish, and to trust in them.

It is vanity also to be ambitious of honors, and to raise one's self to a high station.

It is vanity to follow the lusts of the flesh, and to desire that for which thou must afterwards be grievously punished.

It is vanity to wish for a long life, and to take little care of leading a good life.

It is vanity also to mind this present life, and not to look forward unto those things which are to come.

It is vanity to love that which passeth with all speed, and not to hasten thither where everlasting joy remaineth.

5. Often remember that proverb: "The eye is not satisfied with seeing, nor is the ear filled with hearing." (Eccles. 1:8).

Study, therefore, to withdraw thy heart from the love of visible things, and to turn thyself to things invisible. For they that follow their sensuality, defile their conscience, and lose the grace of God.

CHAPTER II

A Humble Sentiment

ALL men naturally desire to know, but what does knowledge avail without the fear of God?

Indeed an humble husbandman, that serves God, is better than a proud philosopher, who neglecting himself, considers the course of the heavens. (Ecclus. 19:21).

He who knows himself well, is mean in his own eyes, and is not delighted with being praised by men.

If I should know all things that are in the world, and should not be in charity (Rom. 13:8; 1 Cor. 13:2), what would it avail me in the sight of God, who will judge me by my deeds?

2. Leave off that excessive desire of knowing: because there

is found therein much distraction and deceit.

They who are learned, are desirous to appear, and to be called wise.

There are many things, the knowledge of which is of little or no profit to the soul.

And he is very unwise who attends to other things than what may serve to his salvation.

Many words do not satisfy the soul; but a good life gives ease to the mind; and a pure conscience affords a great confidence in God. (1 Tim. 3:9).

3. The more and better thou knowest, the more heavy will be thy judgment unless thy life be also more holy.

Be not, therefore, puffed up with any art or science: but rather fear upon account of the knowledge which is given thee.

If it seem to thee that thou knowest many things, and understandest them well enough, know at the same time, that there are many more things of which thou art ignorant.

Be not high-minded, but rather acknowledge thine ignorance. Why wouldst thou prefer thyself to anyone, since there are many more learned and skillful in the law than thyself?

If thou wouldst know and learn anything to the purpose, love to be unknown and esteemed as nothing.

4. This is the highest science and most profitable lesson, truly to know and despise ourselves.

To have no opinion of ourselves, and to think always well and commendably of others, is great wisdom and high perfection.

If thou shouldst see another openly sin, or commit some heinous crime, yet thou oughtst not to esteem thyself better: because thou knowest not how long thou mayest remain in a good state.

We are all frail: but see thou think no one more frail than thyself.

CHAPTER III
The Doctrine of Truth

HAPPY is he whom Truth teacheth by itself, not by figures and words that pass, but as it is in itself. (Ps. 17:36; Is. 28:26).

Our opinion and our sense often deceive us, and discover but little.

What availeth a great dispute about abstruse and obscure matters, for not knowing which we shall not be questioned at the Day of Judgment?

It is a great folly for us to neglect things profitable and necessary, and willingly to busy ourselves about those which are curious and hurtful. We have eyes and see not. (Ps. 115:5).

2. And what need we concern ourselves about terms of philosophy?

He to whom the eternal Word speaketh, is set at liberty from a multitude of opinions.

From one word are all things, and this one all things speak; and this is the beginning which also speaketh to us.

Without this word, no one understands or judges rightly.

He to whom all things are one, and who draws all things to one, and who sees all things in one, may be steady in heart, and peaceably repose in God. (1 Cor. 2:2).

O Truth! my God, make me one with Thee in eternal love. (John 17:21).

I am wearied with often reading and hearing many things; in Thee is all that I will or desire.

Let all teachers hold their peace; let all creatures be silent in Thy sight; speak Thou alone to me.

3. The more a man is united within himself and interiorly

simple, the more and higher things doth he understand without labour, because he receiveth the light of understanding from above.

A pure, simple, and steady spirit is not dissipated by a multitude of affairs, because he performs them all to the honor of God, and endeavors to be at rest within himself, and free from all self-seeking.

What is a greater hindrance and trouble to thee than thine own unmortified affection of heart?

A good and devout man first disposes his works inwardly which he is to do outwardly.

Neither do they draw him to the desires of an inordinate inclination, but he bends them to the rule of right reason. Who hath a stronger conflict than he who striveth to overcome himself?

And this must be our business, to strive to overcome ourselves, and daily to gain strength over ourselves, and to grow better and better.

4. All perfections in this life are attended with some imperfections, and all our speculations with a certain obscurity.

The humble knowledge of thyself is a surer way to God than the deepest search after science.

Learning is not to be blamed, nor the mere knowledge of anything, which is good in itself, and ordained by God; but a good conscience, and a virtuous life, are always to be preferred before it.

But because many make it more their study to know than to live well, therefore are they often deceived, and bring forth none, or very little fruit.

5. Oh, if men would use as much diligence in rooting out vices and planting virtues, as they do in proposing questions, there would not be so great evils committed, nor scandals among the people, nor so much relaxation in monasteries.

Verily, when the Day of Judgment comes, we shall not be examined on what we have read, but what we have done; nor how learnedly we have spoken, but how religiously we have lived.

Tell me where are now all those great doctors, with whom thou wast well acquainted, whilst they were living and flourished in learning?

Now others fill their places, and I know not whether they ever think of them.

In their lifetime they seemed to be something, and now they are not spoken of.

6. Oh, how quickly doth the glory of the world pass away! (1 John 2:17). Would that their lives had been answerable to their learning! then would they have studied and read well.

How many perish in the world through vain learning, who little care for the service of God!

And because they chose rather to be great than to be humble, therefore they are lost in their own imaginations.

He is truly great, who is great in charity.

He is truly great, who is little in his own eyes, and holdeth as naught the pinnacle of honor.

He is truly prudent who looks upon all earthly things as nothing, that he may gain Christ. (Phil. 3:8).

And he is very learned indeed, who does the will of God, and renounces his own will.

CHAPTER IV

Prudence in Our Doings

WE must not be easy in giving credit to every word and suggestion; but carefully and leisurely weigh the matter according to God.

Alas! such is our weakness, that we often more readily

believe and speak of another that which is evil than that which is good.

But perfect men do not easily give credit to every report, because they know a man's weakness, which is very prone to evil, and very subject to fail in words.

2. It is great wisdom not to be rash in our doings, nor to maintain too obstinately our own opinion:

Nor should we believe every man's word, nor presently tell others the things which we have heard or believed.

Consult with a wise and conscientious man (Tobias 4:19), and seek rather to be instructed by one who is better, than to follow thine own inventions.

A good life makes a man wise according to God, and expert in many things. The more humble a man is in himself, and more subject to God, the more wise will he be in all things, and the more at peace.

CHAPTER V

The Holy Scriptures

TRUTH is to be sought for in Holy Scripture, not eloquence. All Holy Scripture ought to be read with that spirit with which it was made.

We must rather seek for profit in the Scriptures than for subtlety of speech.

We ought as willingly to read devout and simple books, as those that are high and profound.

Let not the authority of the writer offend thee, whether he was of little or of great learning; but let the love of pure truth lead thee to read.

Inquire not who said this; but attend to what is said.

2. Men pass away; "but the truth of the Lord remaineth forever." (Ps. 116:2).

God speaks many ways to us, without respect of persons.

Our curiosity often hinders us in reading the Scriptures, when we attempt to understand and discuss that which should be simply passed over.

If thou wilt receive profit, read with humility, simplicity and faith; and seek not at any time the fame of being learned.

Willingly inquire after, and hear with silence the words of the saints; and be pleased with the parables of the ancients, for they are not spoken without cause. (Ecclus. 32:9).

CHAPTER VI

Inordinate Affections

WHENSOEVER a man desires any thing inordinately, he is presently disquieted within himself.

The proud and covetous are never easy.

The poor and humble of spirit live in much peace.

The man that is not yet perfectly dead to himself, is soon tempted and overcome with small and trifling things.

He that is weak in spirit, and in a manner yet carnal and inclined to sensible things, can hardly withdraw himself wholly from earthly desires.

And therefore he is often sad, when he withdraws himself from them, and is easily moved to anger if anyone thwarts him.

2. And if he has pursued his inclination, he is immediately tormented with the guilt of his conscience, because he has followed his passion, which helps him not at all toward the peace he sought for.

It is then by resisting our passions, that we are to find true peace of heart, and not by being slaves to them.

There is no peace, therefore, in the heart of a carnal man,

nor in a man that is addicted to outward things; but only in a fervent spiritual man.

CHAPTER VII
Flying Vain Hope and Pride

H E is vain who puts his trust in men, or in creatures. (Jer. 17:5; Ps. 114:24).

Be not ashamed to serve others, and to appear poor in this world, for the love of Jesus Christ. (2 Cor. 4:5).

Confide not in thyself; but place thy hope in God. (Ps. 72:28).

Do what is in thy power, and God will be with thy good will.

Trust not in thine own knowledge, nor in the cunning of any man living; but rather in the grace of God, who helps the humble, and humbles those who presume on themselves.

2. Glory not in riches, if thou hast them, nor in friends, because they are powerful; but in God, who gives all things, and desires to give Himself above all things. (1 Cor. 1:31).

Boast not of the stature nor beauty of thy body, which is spoiled and disfigured by a little sickness.

Do not take a pride in thine ability or talent, lest thou displease God, to whom appertaineth every natural good quality and talent which thou hast.

3. Esteem not thyself better than others, lest, perhaps, thou be accounted worse in the sight of God, who knows what is in man.

Be not proud of thine own works; for the judgments of God are different from the judgments of men; and often times, that displeaseth Him which pleaseth men.

If thou hast anything of good, believe better things of others, that thou mayest preserve humility.

It will do thee no harm to esteem thyself the worst of all; but it will hurt thee very much to prefer thyself before anyone.

Continual peace is with the humble; but in the heart of the proud is frequent envy and indignation.

CHAPTER VIII
Shunning Familiarity

"OPEN not thy heart to every man" (Ecclus. 8:22), but treat of thine affairs with a man that is wise and feareth God.

Keep not much company with young people and strangers.

Be not a flatterer with the rich, nor willingly appear before the great.

Associate thyself with the humble and simple, with the devout and virtuous; and treat of those things which edify. (Rom. 14:19).

Be not familiar with any woman; but recommend all good women in general to God.

Desire to be familiar only with God and His angels, and fly the acquaintance of men.

2. We must have charity for all, but familiarity is not expedient.

It sometimes happens that a person, when not known, shines by a good reputation, who, when he is present, is disagreeable to them that see him.

We think sometimes to please others by being with them, and we begin rather to disgust them, by the evil behaviour which they discover in us.

CHAPTER IX

Obedience and Subjection

IT is a very great thing to stand in obedience, to live under a superior, and not be at our own disposal.

It is much more secure to be in a state of subjection than in authority.

Many are under obedience, more out of necessity than for the love of God; and such as these are in pain, and easily repine.

Nor will they gain freedom of mind, unless they submit themselves, with their whole heart, for God's sake.

Run here or there, thou wilt find no rest, but in an humble subjection under the government of a superior.

The imagination and changing of places has deceived many.

2. It is true, everyone is desirous of acting according to his own liking, and is more inclined to such as are of his own mind.

But if God be amongst us, we must sometimes give up our own opinion for the sake of peace.

Who is so wise as to be able fully to know all things?

Therefore trust not too much to thine own thoughts, but be willing also to hear the sentiments of others.

Although thine opinion be good, yet if for God's sake thou leave it to follow that of another, it will be more profitable to thee.

3. For I have often heard, that it is more safe to hear and to take counsel than to give it.

It may also happen that each one's thought may be good, but to refuse to yield to others, when reason or a just cause requires it, is a sign of pride and willfulness.

CHAPTER X
Avoiding Superfluity of Words

FLY the tumult of men as much as thou canst, for treating of worldly affairs hinders very much, although they be discoursed of with a simple intention.

For we are quickly defiled and ensnared with vanity.

I could wish I had oftener been silent, and that I had not been in company.

But why are we so willing to talk and discourse with one another, since we seldom return to silence without prejudice to our conscience.

The reason why we are so willing to talk is, because by discoursing together we seek comfort from one another, and would gladly ease the heart, wearied by various thoughts.

And we very willingly talk and think of such things as we most love and desire, or which we imagine contrary to us.

2. But, alas! it is often in vain and to no purpose, for this outward consolation is no small hindrance to interior and divine comfort.

Therefore we must watch and pray (Matt. 26:41), that our time may not pass away without fruit.

If it be lawful and expedient to speak, speak those things which may edify.

A bad custom, and the neglect of our spiritual advancement, is a great cause of our keeping so little guard upon our mouth.

But devout conferences, concerning spiritual things, help very much to spiritual progress, especially where persons of the same mind and spirit are associated together in God.

CHAPTER XI
Acquiring Peace and Zeal

WE might have much peace if we would not busy ourselves with the sayings and doings of others, and with things which belong not to us.

How can he remain long in peace who entangles himself with other people's cares: who seeks occasions abroad, and who is little or seldom inwardly recollected?

Blessed are the single-hearted, for they shall enjoy much peace.

2. What was the reason why some of the saints were so perfect and contemplative?

Because they made it their study wholly to mortify in themselves all earthly desires; and thus they were enabled, with every fiber of the heart, to cleave to God, and freely to attend to themselves.

We are too much taken up with our own passions; and too solicitous about transitory things.

And seldom do we perfectly overcome so much as one vice, nor are we earnestly bent upon our daily progress; and therefore we remain cold and tepid.

3. If we were perfectly dead to ourselves, and no ways entangled in our interior, then might we be able to relish things divine, and experience something of heavenly contemplation.

The whole and greatest hindrance is, that we are not free from passions and lusts, and strive not to walk in the perfect way of the saints.

And when we meet with any small adversity, we are too quickly dejected, and turn away to seek after human consolation.

4. If we strove like valiant men to stand up in the battle, doubtless we should see Our Lord help us from Heaven.

For He is ready to help them that fight and trust in His grace: who furnishes us with occasions of combat that we may overcome.

If we place our progress in religion in these outward observances only, our devotion will quickly be at an end.

But let us lay the axe to the root, that, being purged from passions, we may possess a quiet mind.

5. If every year we rooted out one vice, we should soon become perfect men.

But now we often find it quite otherwise: that we were better and more pure in the beginning of our conversion, than after many years of our profession.

Our fervor and progress ought to be every day greater; but now it is esteemed a great matter if a man can retain some part of his first fervour.

If we would use but a little violence upon ourselves in the beginning, we might afterwards do all things with ease and joy.

6. It is hard to leave off our old customs; but harder to go against our own will.

But if thou dost not overcome things that are small and light, when wilt thou overcome greater difficulties?

Resist thine inclination in the beginning, and break off thine evil habit, lest perhaps by little and little the difficulty increase upon thee.

Oh, if thou wert sensible how much peace thou shouldst procure to thyself, and joy to others, by behaving thyself well, thou wouldst be more solicitous for thy spiritual progress.

CHAPTER XII

Advantage of Adversity

IT is good for us to have sometimes troubles and adversities, for they make a man enter into himself, that he may know that he is in a state of banishment, and may not place his hopes in anything of this world.

It is good that we sometimes suffer contradictions, and that men have an evil or imperfect opinion of us, even when we do and intend well. These things are often helps to humility, and defend us from vainglory.

For then we better run to God, our inward witness, when outwardly we are despised by men, and little credit is given to us.

2. Therefore should a man so establish himself in God, as to have no need of seeking many comforts from men.

When a man of good will is troubled, or tempted, or afflicted with evil thoughts, then he better understands what need he has of God, without whom he finds he can do no good. (John 15:5).

Then also he laments, he sighs, and prays, by reason of the miseries which he suffers.

Then he is weary of living longer, and he wishes death to come, that he may be "dissolved and be with Christ." (Phil. 1:23).

Then also he will perceive that perfect security and full peace cannot be found in this world.

CHAPTER XIII
Resisting Temptation

AS long as we live in this world we cannot be without tribulation and temptation. Hence it is written in Job: "The life of man upon earth is a warfare." (Job 7:1).

Therefore ought everyone to be solicitous about his temptations, and to watch in prayer, lest the devil, who never sleeps, but "goeth about seeking whom he may devour," find room to deceive him. (1 Ptr. 5:8).

No man is so perfect and holy as not to have sometimes temptations, and we cannot be wholly without them.

2. Yet temptations are often very profitable to a man, although they be troublesome and grievous, for in them a man is humbled, purified, and instructed.

All the saints have passed through many tribulations and temptations, and have profited by them; and they who could not support temptations, have become reprobates, and fallen away.

There is no order so holy, nor place so retired, where there are not temptations and adversities.

3. A man is never entirely secure from temptations as long as he lives, because we have within us the source of temptation, having been born in concupiscence.

When one temptation or tribulation is over, another comes on; and we shall have always something to suffer, because we have lost the good of our original happiness.

Many seek to fly temptations, and fall more grievously into them.

By flight alone we cannot overcome; but by patience and true humility we are made stronger than our enemies.

He who only declines them outwardly, and does not pluck out the root, will profit little; nay, temptations will sooner return to him, and he will find himself in a worse condition.

By degrees, and by patience, with longanimity, thou shalt by God's grace better overcome them than by harshness and thine own importunity.

In temptation often take counsel, and deal not roughly with one that is tempted; but comfort him as thou wouldst wish to be done to thyself.

4. Inconstancy of mind, and small confidence in God, is the beginning of all evil temptations.

For as a ship without a rudder is tossed to and fro by the waves, so the man who is remiss, and who quits his resolution, is many ways tempted.

Fire tries iron, and temptation tries a just man.

We often know not what we can do; but temptation discovers what we are.

However, we must be watchful, especially in the beginning of temptation, because then the enemy is easier overcome, if he is not suffered to come in at all at the door of the soul, but is kept out and resisted at his first knock.

Whence a certain man said: "Withstand the beginning, after-remedies come too late."

For first a bare thought comes to the mind; then a strong imagination; afterwards delight, and evil motion and consent.

And thus, by little and little, the wicked enemy gets full entrance, when he is not resisted in the beginning.

And the longer a man is negligent in resisting, so much the weaker does he daily become in himself, and the enemy becomes stronger against him.

5. Some suffer great temptations in the beginning of their conversion, and some in the end.

And some there are who are much troubled, in a manner, all their lifetime.

Some are but lightly tempted, according to the wisdom and equity of the ordinance of God, who weighs the state and merits of men, and pre-ordains all for the salvation of the elect.

6. We must not, therefore, despair when we are tempted, but pray to God with so much the more fervour that He may vouchsafe to help us in all tribulations; who, no doubt, according to the saying of St. Paul, will "make such issue with the temptation, that you may be able to bear it." (7 Cor. 10:13).

Let us, therefore, humble our souls under the hand of God in all temptations and tribulations: for the humble in spirit He will save and exalt.

7. In temptations and tribulations a man is proved as to what progress he has made; and in them there is a greater merit, and his virtue appears more conspicuous.

Nor is it much if a man be devout and fervent when he feels no trouble; but if in the time of adversity he bears up with patience, there will be hope of a great advancement.

Some are preserved from great temptations, and are often overcome in little daily ones; that, being humbled, they may never presume on themselves in great things, who are weak in such small occurrences.

CHAPTER XIV
Avoiding Judgment

TURN thine eyes back upon thyself, and see thou judge not the doings of others. In judging others, a man labours in vain, often errs, and easily sins; but in judging and looking into himself, he always labours with fruit.

We frequently judge of a thing according as we have it at heart: for we easily lose true judgment through a private affection.

If God were always the only object of our desire, we would not so easily be disturbed at the resistance of our opinions.

2. But often something lies hid within, or occurs without, which draws us along with it.

Many secretly seek themselves in what they do, and are not sensible of it.

They seem also to continue in good peace, when things are done according to their will and judgment; but if it fall out contrary to their desires, they are soon moved, and become sad.

Difference of thoughts and opinions is too frequently the source of dissensions amongst friends and neighbours, amongst religious and devout persons.

3. An old custom is with difficulty relinquished; and no man is led willingly farther than he himself sees or likes.

If thou reliest more upon thine own reason or industry than upon the virtue that subjects to Jesus Christ, thou wilt seldom and hardly be an enlightened man, for God will have us to be perfectly subject to Himself, and to transcend all reason by inflamed love.

CHAPTER XV
Works of Charity

EVIL ought not to be done, either for anything in the world, or for the love of any man, but for the profit of one that stands in need a good work is sometimes freely to be omitted, or rather to be changed for a better.

For by so doing a good work is not lost, but is changed into a better.

Without charity the outward work profiteth nothing; but whatever is done out of charity, be it ever so little and contemptible, all becomes fruitful. (1 Cor. 13:3).

For God regards more with how much affection and love a person performs a work, than how much he does. (Luke 7:47).

2. He does much who loves much.

He does much, that does well what he does.

He does well who regards rather the common good than his own will.

That seems often to be charity which is rather natural affection; because our own natural inclination, self-will, hope of reward, desire of our own interest, will seldom be wanting.

3. He that has true and perfect charity, seeks himself in no one thing, but desires only the glory of God, in all things.

He envies no man, because he loves no private joy; nor does he desire to rejoice in himself: but above all things, he wishes to be made happy in God.

He attributes nothing good to any man, but refers it totally to God, from whom all things proceed as from their fountain, in the enjoyment of whom all the saints repose as in their last end.

Ah! if a man had but one spark of perfect charity, he would doubtless perceive that all earthly things are full of vanity.

CHAPTER XVI
Bearing the Defects of Others

WHAT a man cannot amend in himself or others, he must bear with patience, till God ordains otherwise.

Think that perhaps it is better so, for thy trial and patience, without which our merits are little worth.

Thou must, nevertheless, under such impediments, earnestly pray that God may vouchsafe to help thee, and that thou mayest bear them well.

2. If anyone being once or twice admonished, does not comply, contend not with him, but commit all to God, that His will may be done, and He be honoured in all His servants, who knows well how to convert evil into good.

Endeavour to be patient in supporting the defects and infirmities of others, of what kind soever; because thou also hast many things which others must bear withal.

If thou canst not make thyself such a one as thou wouldst, how canst thou expect to have another according to thy liking?

We would willingly have others perfect, and yet we mend not our own defects.

3. We would have others strictly corrected, but are not willing to be corrected ourselves.

The large liberty of others displeases us, and yet we would not be denied anything we asked for.

We are willing that others should be bound up by laws, and we suffer not ourselves by any means to be restrained.

Thus it is evident how seldom we weigh our neighbour in the same balance with ourselves.

If all were perfect, what then should we have to suffer from others, for God's sake?

4. But now God has so disposed things that we may learn to bear one another's burdens (Gal. 6:2); for there is no man without defect, no man without his burden, no man sufficient for himself, no man wise enough for himself; but we must support one another, comfort one another, assist, instruct, and admonish one another.

But how great each one's virtue is best appears by occasions of adversity; for occasions do not make a man frail, but show what he is.

CHAPTER XVII

A Monastic Life

THOU must learn to renounce thine own will in many things, if thou wilt keep peace and concord with others.

It is no small matter to live in a monastery, or in a congregation, and to converse therein without reproof, and to persevere faithful till death. (Matt. 10:22).

Blessed is he who has there lived well, and made a happy end.

If thou wilt stand as thou oughtest, and make a due progress, look upon thyself as a banished man, and a stranger upon earth. (Heb. 11:13).

Thou must be content to be made a fool for Christ, if thou wilt lead a religious life.

2. The habit and the tonsure contribute little; but a change of manners, and an entire mortification of the passions, make a truly religious man.

He that seeks here any other thing, than purely God and the salvation of his soul, will find nothing but trouble and sorrow.

Neither can he long remain in peace, who does not strive to be the least, and subject to all.

3. Thou camest hither to serve, not to govern; know that thou art called to suffer and to labour, not to idle and to talk.

Here, then, men are tried, as gold in the furnace.

Here no man can stand, unless he be willing, with all his heart to humble himself, for the love of God.

CHAPTER XVIII
Examples of the Holy Fathers

LOOK upon the lively examples of the holy Fathers, in whom true perfection and religion were most shining, and thou wilt see how little, and almost nothing, that is which we do.

Alas! what is our life, if compared to theirs?

The saints and friends of Christ served the Lord in hunger and thirst, in cold and nakedness, in labour and weariness, in watchings and fastings, in prayers and holy meditations, in persecutions and many reproaches. (Heb. 11:37).

2. Ah! how many and how grievous tribulations have the Apostles, martyrs, confessors, virgins, and all the rest undergone, who have been willing to follow Christ's footsteps!

For they hated their lives in this world, that they might possess them for eternity. (John 12:25).

Oh, how strict and mortified a life did the holy Fathers lead in the desert! What long and grievous temptations did they endure! How often were they molested by the enemy! What frequent and fervent prayers did they offer to God! What rigorous abstinence did they go through! What great zeal and fervour had they for their spiritual progress! How strong a war did they wage for overcoming vice! How pure and upright was their intention to God!

They laboured all the day, and in the night they gave themselves to prayer: though even whilst they were at work they ceased not from mental prayer.

3. They spent all their time profitably: every hour seemed short which they spent with God, and through the great sweetness of divine contemplation they forgot even the necessity of their bodily refreshment.

They renounced all riches, dignities, honours, friends, and kindred; they desired to have nothing of this world; they scarcely allowed themselves the necessaries of life; the serving the body, even in necessity, was irksome to them.

They were poor, therefore, as to earthly things, but very rich in grace and virtue.

Outwardly they were in want, but inwardly they were refreshed with divine graces and consolations.

4. They were strangers to the world, but near and familiar friends to God.

They seemed to themselves as nothing, and were despised by this world; but in the eyes of God they were very precious and beloved.

They stood in true humility, they lived in simple obedience, they walked in charity and patience; and therefore they daily advanced in spirit, and obtained great favour with God.

They were given as an example for all religious, and ought more to excite us to make good progress, than the number of the lukewarm to grow slack.

5. Oh, how great was the fervour of all religious in the beginning of their holy institution!

Oh, how great was their devotion in prayer! How great their zeal for virtue! What great discipline was in force among them! What great reverence and obedience in all, flourished under the rule of a superior!

The footsteps remaining, still bear witness that they were truly perfect and holy men, who, waging war so stoutly, trod the world under their feet.

Now he is thought great who is not a transgressor, and who can with patience endure what he hath undertaken.

6. Ah, the lukewarmness and negligence of our state, that we so quickly fall away from our former fervour, and are now even weary of living through sloth and tepidity.

Would to God that advancement in virtues was not wholly asleep in thee who hast so often seen many examples of the devout!

CHAPTER XIX

Excercises of a Religious Man

THE life of a good religious man ought to be eminent in all virtues, that he may be such interiorly as he appears to men in his exterior.

And with good reason ought he to be much more in his interior than he exteriorly appears; because He who beholds us is God, of whom we ought exceedingly to stand in awe, wherever we are, and like angels walk pure in His sight.

We ought every day to renew our resolution, and excite ourselves to fervour as if this were the first day of our conversion, and to say:

Help me, O Lord God, in my good resolution and in Thy holy service, and give me grace now this day perfectly to begin, for what I have hitherto done is nothing.

2. According as our resolution is will the progress of our advancement be; and he hath need of much diligence who would advance much.

Now, if he that makes a strong resolution often fails, what will he do who seldom or but weakly resolves?

The falling off from our resolution happens divers ways, and a small omission in our exercises seldom passeth without some loss.

The resolutions of the just depend on the grace of God, rather than on their own wisdom; and in Him they always put their trust, whatever they take in hands:

For man proposes, but God disposes, nor is the way of man in his own hands. (Prov. 14:12).

3. If for piety's sake, or with a design to the profit of our brother, we sometimes omit our accustomed exercises it may afterwards be easily recovered.

But if, through a loathing of mind, or negligence, it be lightly passed over it is no small fault and will prove hurtful. With our utmost endeavours we will still be apt to fail in many things.

But we must always resolve on something certain, and in particular against those things which hinder us most.

We must examine and order well both our exterior and interior; because both conduce to our advancement.

4. If thou canst not continually recollect thy self do it sometimes, and at least once a day, that is, at morning or evening.

In the morning resolve, in the evening examine thy performances, how thou hast behaved this day in word, work, or thought; because in these, perhaps, thou hast often offended God and thy neighbour.

Prepare thyself like a man to resist the wicked attacks of the devil; bridle gluttony, and thou shalt the easier restrain all carnal inclinations.

Be never altogether idle, but either reading or writing, or praying or meditating, or labouring in something that may be for the common good.

Yet in bodily exercises a discretion is to be used; nor are they equally to be undertaken by all.

5. Those things which are not common are not to be done in public, for particular things are more safely done in private.

But take care thou be not backward in common exercises and more forward in things of thine own particular devotion; but having fully and faithfully performed what thou art bound to, and what is enjoined thee, if thou hast any time remaining, give thyself to thyself according as thy devotion shall incline thee.

All cannot have the self-same exercise; but this is more proper for one and that for another.

Moreover, according to the diversity of times, divers exercises are more pleasing; for some relish better on festival days, others on common days.

We stand in need of one kind in time of temptation, and of another in time of peace and rest.

Some we willingly think on when we are sad, others when we are joyful in the Lord.

6. About the time of the principal festivals we must renew our good exercises and more fervently implore the prayers of the saints.

We ought to make our resolution from festival to festival, as if we were then to depart out of this world, and to come to the everlasting festival.

Therefore we ought carefully to prepare ourselves at times of devotion, and to converse more devoutly, and to keep all observances more strictly, as being shortly to receive the reward of our labour from God.

7. And if it be deferred, let us believe that we are not well prepared and that we are as yet unworthy of the great glory which shall be revealed to us at the appointed time (Rom. 7:18); and let us endeavour to prepare ourselves better for our departure.

Blessed is that servant, says the Evangelist St. Luke (Luke 12:57), whom, when his Lord shall come he shall find watching. Amen, I say to you, he shall set him over all his possessions.

CHAPTER XX
Love of Solitude and Silence

SEEK a proper time to retire into thyself, and often think of the benefits of God.

Let curiosities alone.

Read such matters as may rather move thee to compunction than give thee occupation.

If thou wilt withdraw thyself from superfluous talk and idle visits, as also from giving ear to news and to reports, thou wilt find time sufficient and proper to employ thyself in good meditations.

The greatest saints avoided the company of men as much as they could and chose to live to God in secret.

2. "As often as I have been amongst men," said a philosopher, "I have returned less a man"; this we often experience when we talk long.

It is easier to be altogether silent than not to exceed in words.

It is easier to keep retired at home than to be able to be sufficiently upon one's guard abroad.

Whosoever, therefore, aims at arriving at internal and spiritual things, must, with Jesus, go aside from the crowd. (John 5:13).

No man is secure in appearing abroad, but he who would willingly lie hid at home.

No man securely speaks but he who loves to hold his peace.

No man securely governs but he who would willingly live in subjection.

No man securely commands but he who has learned well to obey.

3. No man securely rejoiceth unless he hath within him the testimony of a good conscience. (2 Cor. 1:12).

Yet the security of the saints was always full of the fear of God.

Neither were they less careful or humble in themselves, because they were shining with great virtues and graces.

But the security of the wicked arises from pride and presumption, and will end in deceiving themselves.

Never promise thyself security in this life, though thou seem to be a good religious man, or a devout hermit.

4. Oftentimes they that were better in the judgment of men have been in greater danger by reason of their too great confidence.

So that it is better for many not to be altogether free from temptations but to be often assaulted; that they may not be too secure lest, perhaps, they be lifted up with pride, or take more liberty to go aside after exterior comforts.

Oh, how good a conscience would that man preserve, who would never seek after transitory joy, nor ever busy himself with the world!

Oh, how great peace and tranquillity would he possess, who would cut off all vain solicitude, and only think of the things of God, and his salvation, and place his whole hope in God!

5. No man is worthy of heavenly comfort who has not diligently exercised himself in holy compunction.

If thou wouldst find compunction in thy heart retire into thy chamber and shut out the tumult of the world, as it is written: "Have compunction in your chambers." (Ps. 4:5). Thou shalt find in thy cell what thou shalt often lose abroad.

Thy cell, if thou continue in it, grows sweet; but if thou keep not to it, it becomes tedious and distasteful. If in the beginning of thy conversion thou accustom thyself to remain in thy cell and keep it well, it will be to thee afterwards a dear friend and a most agreeable delight.

6. In silence and quiet the devout soul goes forward and learns the secrets of the Scriptures.

There she finds floods of tears, with which she may wash and cleanse herself every night, that she may become the more familiar with her Maker, by the farther she lives from all worldly tumult. (Ps. 6).

For God with His holy angels will draw nigh to him who withdraws himself from his acquaintances and friends.

It is better to lie hidden and take care of one's self than neglecting one's self to work even miracles.

It is commendable for a religious man to go seldom abroad, to fly being seen, and not desire to see men.

7. Why wilt thou see what thou must not have? "The world passeth away, and the concupiscence thereof." (1 John 2:17).

The desires of sensuality draw thee abroad, but when the hour is past what dost thou bring home but a weight upon thy conscience and a dissipation of heart.

A joyful going abroad often brings forth a sorrowful coming home; and a merry evening makes a sad morning.

So all carnal joys enter pleasantly but in the end bring remorse and death.

What canst thou see elsewhere which thou seest not here? Behold the heavens and the earth, and all the elements; for of these are all things made.

8. What canst thou see anywhere which can continue long under the sun?

Thou thinkest perhaps to be satisfied, but thou canst not attain to it.

If thou couldst see all things at once before thee what would it be but a vain sight? (Eccles. 1:14)

Lift up thine eyes to God on high and pray for thy sins and negligences. (Eccles. 3:4; Ps. 122:1).

Leave vain things to vain people, but mind thou the things which God hath commanded thee.

Shut thy door upon thee, and call to thee Jesus thy beloved.

Stay with Him in thy cell, for thou shalt not find such great peace anywhere else.

If thou hadst not gone abroad, nor hearkened to rumours, thou hadst kept thyself better in good peace; but since thou art delighted sometimes to hear news thou must thence suffer a disturbance of heart.

CHAPTER XXI

Compunction of Heart

IF thou wilt make any progress keep thyself in the fear of God (Prov. 23:17), and be not too free, but restrain all thy senses under discipline, and give not thyself up to foolish mirth.

Give thyself to compunction of heart and thou shalt find devotion.

Compunction opens the way to much good, which dissolution is wont quickly to lose.

It is wonderful that any man can heartily rejoice in this life who weighs and considers his banishment and the many dangers of his soul.

2. Through levity of heart and the little thought we have of our defects we feel not the sorrows of our soul, but often vainly laugh when in all reason we ought to weep.

There is no true liberty, nor solid joy, but in the fear of God with a good conscience.

Happy is he who can cast away all impediments of distractions and recollect himself to the union of holy compunction.

Happy is he who separates himself from all that may burden or defile his conscience.

Strive manfully; custom is overcome by custom.

If thou canst let men alone they will let thee do what thou hast to do.

3. Busy not thyself with other men's affairs, nor entangle thyself with the causes of great people.

Have always an eye upon thyself in the first place and take special care to admonish thyself preferably to all thy dearest friends.

If thou hast not the favour of men be not grieved thereat: but let thy concern be that thou dost not carry thyself so well and so circumspectly as it becomes a servant of God, and a devout religious man to demean himself.

It is oftentimes more profitable and more secure for a man not to have many comforts in this life, especially according to the flesh.

Yet, that we have not divine comforts, or seldomer experience them, is our own fault, because we do not seek compunction of heart, nor cast off altogether vain and outward satisfactions.

4. Acknowledge thyself unworthy of divine consolation, and rather worthy of much tribulation.

When a man has perfect compunction then the whole world is to him burdensome and distasteful.

A good man always finds subjects enough for mourning and weeping.

For whether he considers himself, or thinks of his neighbour, he knows that no man lives here without tribulation; and the more thoroughly he considers himself, the more he grieves.

The subjects for just grief and interior compunction are our vices and sins, in which we lie entangled in such a manner as seldom to be able to contemplate heavenly things.

5. If thou wouldst oftener think of thy death than of a long life, no doubt thou wouldst more fervently amend thyself.

And if thou didst seriously consider in thy heart the future punishment of Hell or Purgatory, I believe thou wouldst willingly endure labour and pain, and fear no kind of austerity.

But because these things reach not the heart, and we still love the things which flatter us, therefore we remain cold and very sluggish.

6. It is oftentimes a want of spirit which makes the wretched body so easily complain.

Pray, therefore, humbly to Our Lord, that He may give thee the spirit of compunction, and say with the Prophet, "Feed me, O Lord, with the bread of tears and give me drink of tears in measure." (Ps. 79:6).

CHAPTER XXII

The Misery of Man

THOU art miserable wherever thou art, and which way soever thou turnest thyself, unless thou dost turn thyself to God.

Why art thou troubled because things do not succeed with thee according to thy will and desire? Who is there that has all things according to his will! Neither I, nor thou, nor any man upon earth.

There is no man in the world without some trouble or affliction, though he be a king or a pope.

Who is it that is most at ease? Doubtless he who is willing to suffer something for God's sake.

2. Many unstable and weak men are apt to say: Behold how well such a man lives; how rich, how great, how mighty and powerful.

But attend to heavenly goods and thou wilt see that all these temporal things are nothing but very uncertain and rather burdensome, because they are never possessed without care and fear.

The happiness of a man consisteth not in having temporal things in abundance, but a moderate competency sufficeth.

It is truly a misery to live upon earth.

The more a man desireth to be spiritual, the more this present life becomes distasteful to him, because he the better understands and more clearly sees the defects of human corruption.

For to eat, drink, watch, sleep, rest, labour, and to be subject to other necessities of nature, is truly a great misery and affliction to a devout man who desires to be released and free from all sin.

3. For the inward man is very much burdened with the necessities of the body in this world.

And, therefore, the Prophet devoutly prays to be freed from them, saying, "From my necessities deliver me, O Lord." (Ps. 24:17).

But woe to them that know not their own misery, and more woe to them that love this miserable and corruptible life.

For some there are that love it to that degree, although they can scarce get necessaries by labouring or begging, that if they could live always here they would not care at all for the Kingdom of God.

4. O senseless people, and infidels in heart, who lie buried so deep in earthly things as to relish nothing but the things of the flesh.

Miserable wretches! they will in the end find to their cost how vile a nothing that was which they so much loved.

But the saints of God and all the devout friends of Christ made no account of what pleased the flesh or flourished in this life; but their whole hope and intention aspired to eternal goods.

Their whole desire tended upwards to things everlasting and invisible, lest the love of visible things should draw them down to things below.

5. Lose not, brother, thy confidence of going forward to spiritual things; there is yet time, the hour is not yet past.

Why wilt thou put off thy resolutions from day to day? Arise, and begin this very moment, and say: now is the time for doing, and now is the time to fight; now is the proper time to amend my life.

When thou art troubled and afflicted then is the time to merit.

Thou must pass through fire and water before thou comest to refreshment. (Ps. 65:12).

Unless thou do violence to thyself thou wilt not overcome vice.

As long as we carry about us this frail body we cannot be without sin nor live without uneasiness and sorrow.

We would fain be at rest from all misery, but because we have lost innocence by sin we have also lost true happiness.

We must, therefore, have patience and wait for the mercy of God till iniquity pass away and this mortality be swallowed up by life. (2 Cor. 5:4).

6. Oh, how great is human frailty, which is always prone to vice!

Today thou confessest thy sins, and tomorrow thou again committest what thou hast confessed.

Now thou resolvest to take care, and an hour after thou dost as if thou hadst never resolved.

We have reason, therefore, to humble ourselves and never to think much of ourselves since we are so frail and inconstant.

That may also be quickly lost through negligence, which, with much labour and time, was hardly gotten by grace.

7. What will become of us yet in the end who grow lukewarm so very soon?

Woe be to us if we are for giving ourselves to rest, as if we had already met with peace and security, when there does not as yet appear any mark of true sanctity in our conversation. (1 Thess. 5:3).

It would be very needful that we should again, like good novices, be instructed in all good behaviour and if so, perhaps there would be some hopes of future amendment and greater spiritual progress.

CHAPTER XXIII

The Thoughts of Death

VERY quickly must thou be gone from hence, see then how matters stand with thee; a man is here today and tomorrow he is vanished. (1 Mach. 2:63).

And when he is taken away from the sight he is quickly also out of mind.

Oh, the dullness and hardness of man's heart, which only thinks of what is present, and looks not forward to things to come.

Thou oughtst in every action and thought so to order thyself as if thou wert immediately to die.

If thou hadst a good conscience thou wouldst not much fear death.

It were better for thee to fly sin than to be afraid of death. (Dan. 13:23).

If thou art not prepared today how shalt thou be tomorrow?

Tomorrow is an uncertain day; and how dost thou know that thou shalt be alive tomorrow? (James 4:14).

2. What benefit is it to live long when we advance so little? Ah! long life does not always make us better, but often adds to our guilt.

Would to God we had behaved ourselves well in this world even for one day!

Many count the years of their conversion; but oftentimes the fruit of amendment is but small.

If it be frightful to die, perhaps it will be more dangerous to live longer.

Blessed is he that has always the hour of death before his eyes and every day disposes himself to die. (Ecclus. 7:40).

If thou hast at any time seen a man die think that thou must also pass the same way.

3. In the morning imagine that thou shalt not live till night; and when evening comes presume not to promise thyself the next morning.

Be therefore always prepared, and live in such a manner that death may never find thee unprovided.

Many die suddenly and when they little think of it: "Because at what hour you know not the Son of man will come." (Matt. 24:44).

When that last hour shall come thou wilt begin to have quite other thoughts of thy whole past life; and thou wilt be exceedingly grieved that thou hast been so negligent and remiss. (Wis. 5:6).

TRUE

4. How happy and prudent is he who strives to be such now in this life as he desires to be found at his death.

For it will give a man a great confidence of dying happily if he has a perfect contempt of the world, a fervent desire of advancing in virtue, a love for discipline, the spirit of penance, a ready obedience, self-denial, and patience in bearing all adversities for the love of Christ.

LOVE

Thou mayest do many good things whilst thou art well,

but when thou art sick I know not what thou wilt be able to do.

Few are improved by sickness; so too they that travel much abroad seldom become holy.

5. Trust not in thy friends and relations, nor put off the welfare of thy soul to hereafter; for men will sooner forget thee than thou imaginest.

It is better now to provide in time, and send some good before thee, than to trust to the help of others after thy death. (Matt. 6:20).

If thou art not now careful for thyself who will be careful for thee hereafter?

The present time is very precious; "Now is the acceptable time: now is the day of salvation." (2 Cor. 6:2).

But it is greatly to be lamented that thou dost not spend this time more profitably in which thou mayest acquire wherewith to live forever.

The time will come when thou wilt wish for one day or hour to amend, and I know not whether thou shalt obtain it.

6. O my dearly beloved, from how great a danger mayest thou deliver thyself! from how great a fear mayest thou be freed if thou wilt but now be always fearful and looking for death!

Strive now so to live that in the hour of thy death thou mayest rather rejoice than fear.

Learn now to die to the world that then thou mayest begin to live with Christ. (Rom. 6:8).

Learn now to despise all things that then thou mayest freely go to Christ.

Chastise thy body now by penance that thou mayest then have an assured confidence. (1 Cor. 9:27).

7. Ah fool! why dost thou think to live long when thou art not sure of one day? (Luke 12:20).

How many thinking to live long have been deceived and unexpectedly snatched away!

How often hast thou heard related that such a man was slain by the sword; another drowned; another falling from on high broke his neck; this man died at the table; that other came to his end when he was at play.

Some have perished by fire, some by the sword, some by pestilence, some by robbers: and thus death is the end of all, and man's life passeth suddenly like a shadow. (Eccles. 7:1).

8. Who will remember thee when thou art dead, and who will pray for thee?

Do now, beloved, do now all thou canst, because thou knowest not when thou shalt die; nor dost thou know what shall befall thee after death.

Whilst thou hast time heap to thyself riches that will never die! (Matt. 6:20).

Think of nothing but thy salvation, care for nothing but the things of God.

Make now to thyself friends, by honouring the saints of God, and imitating their actions, that when thou shalt fail in this life they may receive thee into everlasting dwellings. (Luke 16:9).

9. Keep thyself as a pilgrim, and a stranger upon earth, to whom the affairs of this world do not in the least belong. (1 Ptr. 2:11).

Keep thy heart free and raised upwards to God, because thou hast not here a lasting abode.

Send thither thy daily prayers, with sighs and tears, that after death thy spirit may be worthy to pass happily to Our Lord. Amen.

CHAPTER XXIV
Punishment of Sins

IN all things look to thine end (Ecclus. 7:40), and how thou shalt be able to stand before a severe Judge, from whom nothing is hidden, who takes no bribes, nor receives excuses, but will judge that which is just.

O most wretched and foolish sinner, what answer wilt thou make to God, who knows all thine evils? thou who art sometimes afraid of the looks of an angry man.

Why dost thou not provide for thyself against the Day of Judgment, when no man can be excused or defended by another, but every one shall have enough to do to answer for himself?

At present thy labour is profitable; thy tears are acceptable, thy sighs will be heard, thy sorrow is satisfactory, and may purge away thy sins.

2. A patient man hath a great and wholesome purgatory, who, receiving injuries, is more concerned at the person's sin than his own wrong; who willingly prays for his adversaries, and from his heart forgives offences; who delays not to ask forgiveness of others; who is easier moved to compassion than to anger; who frequently useth violence to himself, and labours to bring the flesh wholly under subjection to the spirit.

It is better now to purge away our sins and to cut up our vices than to reserve them to be purged hereafter.

Truly we deceive ourselves through the inordinate love we bear to our flesh.

3. What other things shall the fire feed on but thy sins?

The more thou sparest thyself now and followest the flesh the more grievously shalt thou suffer hereafter and the more fuel dost thou lay up for that fire.

In those things which a man has more sinned shall he be more heavily punished.

There the slothful shall be pricked forward with burning goads, and the glutton will be tormented with extreme hunger and thirst.

There the luxurious and the lovers of pleasure shall be covered all over with burning pitch and stinking brimstone, and the envious like mad dogs shall howl for grief.

4. There is no vice which will not there have its proper torment.

There the proud shall be filled with all confusion, and the covetous be straitened with most miserable want.

There one hour of suffering will be more sharp than a hundred years here spent in the most rigid penance.

There is no rest, no comfort for the damned; but here there is sometimes intermission of labour, and we receive comfort from our friends.

Be careful at present and sorrowful for thy sins, that in the Day of Judgment thou mayest be secure with the blessed.

"For then shall the just stand with great constancy against those that have afflicted and oppressed them." (Wis. 5:1).

Then will he stand to judge who now humbly submits himself to the judgment of men.

Then the poor and the humble shall have great confidence and the proud shall fear on every side.

5. Then will it appear that he was wise in this world who learned for Christ's sake to be a fool and despised.

Then all tribulation suffered with patience will be pleasing "and all iniquity shall stop her mouth." (Ps. 106:42).

Then every devout person shall rejoice and the irreligious shall be sad.

Then the flesh that has been mortified shall triumph more than if it had always been pampered in delights.

Then shall the mean habit shine and fine clothing appear contemptible.

Then shall the poor cottage be more commended than the gilded palace.

Then constant patience shall more avail than all the power of the world.

Then simple obedience shall be more prized than all worldly craftiness. '

6. Then a pure and good conscience shall be a greater subject of joy than learned philosophy.

Then the contempt of riches shall weigh more than all the treasures of worldlings.

Then wilt thou be more comforted that thou hast prayed devoutly than that thou hast fared daintily.

Then wilt thou rejoice more that thou hast kept silence than that thou hast made long discourses or talked much.

Then will holy works be of greater value than many fair words.

Then will a strict life and hard penance be more pleasing than all the delights of the earth.

Learn, at present, to suffer in little things, that then thou mayest be delivered from more grievous sufferings.

Try first here what thou canst suffer hereafter.

If thou canst now endure so little how wilt thou be able to bear everlasting torments?

If a little suffering now makes thee so impatient what will hellfire do hereafter?

Surely thou canst not have both joys—take thy pleasure in this world and afterwards reign with Christ.

7. If to this day thou hadst always lived in honours and pleasures what would it avail thee if thou wert now in a moment to die?

All then is vanity but to love God and to serve Him alone. (Eccles. 1:2; Deut. 10:20).

For he that loves God with his whole heart neither fears death, nor punishment, nor judgment, nor Hell; because perfect love gives secure access to God.

But he that is yet delighted with sin no wonder if he be afraid of death and judgment.

It is good, however, that if love, as yet, reclaim thee not from evil, at least the fear of Hell restrain thee.

But he that lays aside the fear of God will not be able to continue long in good, but will quickly fall into the snares of the devil.

CHAPTER XXV
Amendment of Our Lives

B E vigilant and diligent in God's service, and often think with thyself to what end thou camest hither, and why thou didst leave the world: Was it not that thou mightest live in God and become a spiritual man?

Be fervent, therefore, in thy spiritual progress, for thou shalt shortly receive the reward of thy labours; and then grief and fear shall no more come near thee.

Thou shalt labour now a little and thou shalt find great rest; yea, everlasting joy.

If thou continue faithful and fervent in working, God will doubtless be faithful and liberal in rewarding.

Thou must preserve a good and firm hope of winning the victory; but must not think thyself secure, lest thou grow negligent or proud.

2. When a certain person in anxiety of mind was often wavering between hope and fear, and, on a time, being overwhelmed with grief, had prostrated himself in prayer in the

church before a certain altar, he revolved these things within himself saying: "If I did but know that I should still persevere"; and presently he heard within himself this answer from God: "And if thou didst know this what wouldst thou do? Do now what thou wouldst then do, and thou shalt be very secure." And immediately, being comforted and strengthened, he committed himself to the divine will, and his anxious wavering ceased.

Neither had he a mind anymore to search curiously, to know what should befall him hereafter; but rather studied to inquire what was the will of God, "well pleasing and perfect" (Rom. 12:2), for the beginning and accomplishment of every good work.

3. "Trust in the Lord, and do good," saith the Prophet, "and dwell in the land, and thou shalt be fed with its riches." (Ps. 36:3).

There is one thing which keeps many back from spiritual progress and fervent amendment of life: and that is, dread of difficulty, or the labour which must be gone through in the conflict.

And they indeed advance most of all others in virtue, who strive manfully to overcome those things which they find more troublesome or contrary to them.

For there a man makes greater progress and merits greater grace where he overcomes himself more and mortifies himself in spirit.

4. But all men have not equal difficulties to overcome and mortify.

Yet he that is diligent and zealous, although he may have more passions to fight against, will be able to make a greater progress than another who has fewer passions but is withal less fervent in the pursuit of virtue.

Two things particularly conduce to a great amendment:

these are, forcibly to withdraw one's self from that to which nature is viciously inclined, and earnestly to labour for that good which one wants most.

Study likewise to fly more carefully and to overcome those faults which most frequently displease thee in others.

5. Turn all occasions to thy spiritual profit: so that if thou see or hear any good examples thou mayest be spurred on to imitate them.

But if thou observe anything that is reprehensible take heed thou commit not the same; or if thou at any time hast done it, labour to amend it quickly.

As thine eye observeth others so art thou also observed by others.

Oh, how sweet and comfortable is it to see brethren fervent and devout, regular and well disciplined! (Ps. 132:1).

How sad a thing and how afflicting to see them walk disorderly, and practice nothing of what they are called to!

How hurtful it is to neglect the intent of our vocation and turn our minds to things that are not our business.

6. Be mindful of the resolution thou hast taken, and set before thee the image of the crucifix.

Well mayest thou be ashamed if thou hast looked upon the life of Jesus Christ, that thou hast not yet studied to conform thyself more to His pattern, although thou hast been long in the way of God.

A religious man, who exercises himself seriously and devoutly in the most holy life and Passion of Our Lord, shall find there abundantly all things profitable and necessary for him; nor need he seek any better model than that of Jesus.

Oh, if our crucified Jesus did but come into our heart, how quickly and sufficiently learned should we be!

7. A fervent religious man bears and takes all things well that are commanded him.

A negligent and lukewarm religious man has trouble upon trouble, and on every side suffers anguish, because he has no comfort within and is hindered from seeking any without.

A religious man that lives not in discipline lies open to dreadful ruin.

He that seeks to be more loose and remiss will always be uneasy, for one thing or other will always displease him.

8. How do so many other religious do who live under strict monastic discipline?

They seldom go abroad, they live very retired, their diet is very poor, their habit coarse, they labor much, they speak little, they watch long, they rise early, they spend much time in prayer, they read often and keep themselves in all discipline.

Consider the Carthusians, the Cistercians, and the monks and nuns of divers Orders, how every night they rise to sing psalms to the Lord.

It would, therefore, be a shame for thee to be sluggish at so holy a time, when such multitudes of religious begin with joy to give praise to God.

9. Oh, that we had nothing else to do but to praise the Lord our God with our whole heart and mouth!

Oh, that thou didst never want to eat, nor drink, nor sleep, but couldst always praise God and be employed solely in spiritual exercises!

Thou wouldst then be much more happy than now whilst thou art under the necessity of serving the flesh.

Would there were no such necessities, but only the spiritual refreshments of the soul, which, alas, we taste too seldom.

10. When a man is come to this, that he seeks comfort from nothing created, then he begins perfectly to relish God; then likewise will he be well content, however matters happen to him.

Then will he neither rejoice for much, nor be sorrowful for little, but will commit himself wholly and confidently to God, who is to him all in all; to whom nothing perishes or dies, but all things live to Him and serve Him at a nod without delay.

11. Always remember thine end and that time once lost never returns. Without care and diligence thou shalt never acquire virtues.

If thou begin to grow lukewarm thou wilt begin to be uneasy.

But if thou give thyself to fervour thou shalt find great peace, and the grace of God and love of virtue will make thee feel less labour.

A fervent and diligent man is ready for all things.

It is a greater task to resist vices and passions than to toil at bodily labours.

He that does not shun small defects by little and little falls into greater. (Ecclus. 19:1).

Thou shalt always rejoice in the evening if thou spend the day profitably.

Watch over thyself, stir up thyself, admonish thyself, and whatever becometh of others neglect not thyself.

The greater violence thou offerest to thyself the greater progress thou shalt make.

BOOK II

ADMONITIONS CONCERNING INTERIOR THINGS

CHAPTER I

Interior Conversation

THE Kingdom of God is within you (Luke 17:21), saith the Lord. Convert thyself with thy whole heart to the Lord (Joel 2:12), and quit this miserable world, and thy soul shall find rest.

Learn to despise exterior things, and give thyself to the interior, and thou shalt see the Kingdom of God will come into thee.

For the Kingdom of God is peace and joy in the Holy Ghost, which is not given to the wicked. (Rom. 14:17).

Christ will come to thee, discovering to thee His consolation, if thou wilt prepare Him a fit dwelling within thee.

All His glory and beauty is in the interior (Ps. 44:14), and there He pleaseth Himself.

Frequently doth He visit the internal man, sweet in His communication with him, delightful His consolation, much peace, and a familiarity exceedingly to be admired.

2. O faithful soul, prepare·thy heart for this thy spouse, that He may vouchsafe to come to thee, and dwell in thee!

For so He saith: "If any man love me he will keep my word, and my Father will love him, and we will come to him, and we will make our abode with him." (John 14:23).

Make room then for Christ within thee and deny entrance to all others.

When thou hast Christ thou art rich and He is sufficient for thee; He will provide for thee, and will be thy faithful procurator in all things, so that thou needst not trust to men.

For men quickly change and presently fail: but Christ remains forever and stands by us firmly to the end.

3. There is no great confidence to be put in a frail mortal

man, though he be profitable and beloved (Ps. 145:2); nor much grief to be taken if sometimes he be against thee and cross thee.

They that are with thee today may be against thee tomorrow; and on the other hand often changed like the wind.

Place thy whole confidence in God and let Him be thy fear and thy love; He will answer for thee and do for thee what is for the best. (Jer. 17:7).

Thou hast not here a lasting city and wherever thou art thou art a stranger and a pilgrim (1 Ptr. 2:11); nor wilt thou ever have rest unless thou be interiorly united to Christ.

4. Why dost thou stand looking about thee here, since this is not thy resting place?

Thy dwelling must be in Heaven, and all things of the earth are only to be looked upon as passing by.

All things pass away and thou along with them. (Wis. 5:9).

See that thou cleave not to them, lest thou be ensnared and be lost.

Let thy thought be with the Most High, and thy prayer directed to Christ without intermission.

If thou knowest not how to meditate on high and heavenly things, rest on the Passion of Christ, and willingly dwell in His sacred Wounds.

For if thou flee devoutly to the Wounds and precious stigmas of Jesus, thou shalt feel great comfort in tribulation; neither wilt thou much regard being despised by men, but wilt easily bear up against detracting tongues.

5. Christ was also in this world despised by men, and in His greatest necessity forsáken by His acquaintance and friends in the midst of reproaches.

Christ would suffer and be despised, and dost thou dare to complain of anyone?

Christ had adversaries and backbiters, and wouldst thou have all to be thy friends and benefactors?

Whence shall thy patience be crowned if thou meet with no adversity?

If thou wilt suffer no opposition, how wilt thou be a friend of Christ?

Suffer with Christ and for Christ if thou desirest to reign with Christ. (2 Tim. 2:12).

6. If thou hadst once perfectly entered into the interior of Jesus and experienced a little of His burning love, then wouldst thou not care at all for thine own convenience or inconvenience, but wouldst rather rejoice at reproach, because the love of Jesus makes a man despise himself.

A lover of Jesus and of truth, and a true internal man, that is free from inordinate affections, can freely turn himself to God and in spirit elevate himself above himself, and rest in enjoyment.

7. He to whom all things relish as they are, not as they are esteemed or said to be, is wise indeed, and taught rather by God than men.

He who knows how to walk internally, and to make little account of external things, is not at a loss for proper places or times for performing devout exercises.

An internal man quickly recollects himself, because he never pours forth his whole self upon outward things.

Exterior labour is no prejudice to him, or any employment which for a time is necessary; but as things fall out, he accommodates himself to them.

He that is well-disposed and orderly in his interior heeds not the strange and perverse carriages of men.

As much as a man draws things to himself, so much is he hindered and distracted by them.

8. If thou hadst a right spirit within thee, and wert well

purified from earthly affections, all things would turn to thy good and to thy profit.

For this reason do many things displease and often trouble thee, because thou art not as yet perfectly dead to thyself, nor separated from all earthly things.

Nothing so defiles and entangles the heart of man as impure love to created things.

If thou reject exterior comfort thou wilt be able to contemplate heavenly things, and frequently to feel excessive joy interiorly.

CHAPTER II

Of Humble Submission

MAKE no great account who is for thee or against thee, but let it be thy business and thy care that God may be with thee in everything thou dost. (Rom. 8:31).

Have a good conscience, and God will sufficiently defend thee.

For he whom God will help no man's malice can hurt.

If thou canst but hold thy peace and suffer, thou shalt see, without doubt, that the Lord will help thee.

He knows the time and manner of delivering thee and therefore thou must resign thyself to Him.

It belongs to God to help and to deliver us from all confusion.

Oftentimes it is very profitable for keeping us in greater humility that others know and reprehend our faults.

2. When a man humbles himself for his defects he then easily appeases others, and quickly satisfies those that are angry with him.

The humble man God protects and delivers; the humble

He loves and comforts; to the humble He inclines Himself; to the humble He gives grace (Prov. 29:23), and after he has been depressed, raises him to glory.

To the humble He reveals His secrets, and sweetly draws and invites him to Himself.

The humble man having received reproach maintains himself well enough in peace, because he is fixed on God, and not on the world.

Never think thou hast made any progress till thou lookest upon thyself as inferior to all.

CHAPTER III

Of a Good Peaceable Man

KEEP thyself first in peace and then thou wilt be able to bring others to peace.

A peaceable man does more good than one that is very learned.

A passionate man turns every good to evil and easily believes evil.

A good peaceable man turns all things to good.

He that is in perfect peace suspects no man, but he that is discontented and disturbed is tossed about with various suspicions; he is neither quiet himself nor does he suffer others to be quiet.

He often says that which he should not say, and omits that which would be better for him to do.

He considers what others are obliged to do, and neglects that to which he himself is obliged.

Have, therefore, a zeal in the first place over thyself, and then thou mayest justly exercise thy zeal towards thy neighbour.

2. Thou knowest well enough how to excuse and colour

thine own doings, and thou wilt not take the excuses of others.

It were more just that thou shouldst accuse thyself and excuse thy brother.

If thou wilt be borne with bear also with another.

See how far thou art yet from true charity and humility, which knows not how to be angry with anyone, or to have indignation against anyone but one's self.

It is no great thing to be able to converse with them that are good and meek, for this is naturally pleasing to all. And everyone would willingly have peace and love those best that agree with them.

But to live peaceably with those that are harsh and perverse, or disorderly, or such as oppose us, is a great grace, and highly commendable and manly.

3. Some there are who keep themselves in peace and have peace also with others.

And there are some that are neither at peace within themselves, nor suffer others to be in peace; they are troublesome to others, but always more troublesome to themselves.

And some there are who keep themselves in peace and study to restore peace to others.

Yet all our peace in this miserable life is rather to be placed in humble sufferings than in not feeling adversities.

He who knows how to suffer will enjoy much peace.

Such a one is a conqueror of himself and lord of the world, a friend of Christ, and an heir of Heaven.

CHAPTER IV

Of a Pure Mind

WITH two wings a man is lifted up above earthly things: that is, with simplicity and purity.

Simplicity must be in the intention, purity in the affection.

Simplicity aims at God, purity takes hold of Him and tastes Him.

No good action will hinder thee if thou be free from inordinate affections.

If thou intend and seek nothing but the will of God and the profit of thy neighbour, thou shalt enjoy eternal liberty.

If thy heart were right, then every creature would be to thee a mirror of life and a book of holy doctrine.

There is no creature so little and contemptible as not to manifest the goodness of God.

2. If thou wert good and pure within, then wouldst thou discern all things without impediment and understand them rightly.

A pure heart penetrates Heaven and Hell.

According as everyone is interiorly, so he judgeth exteriorly.

If there be joy in the world, certainly the man whose heart is pure enjoys it.

And if there be anywhere tribulation and anguish, an evil conscience feels the most of it. (Rom. 2:9).

As iron put into the fire loses the rust and becomes all glowing, so a man that turns himself wholly to God puts off his sluggishness and is changed into a new man.

3. When a man begins to grow lukewarm he is afraid of a little labour and willingly takes external comfort.

But when he begins perfectly to overcome himself and to walk manfully in the way of God, then he makes less account of those things, which before he considered burdensome to him.

CHAPTER V
Consideration of One's Self

WE cannot trust much to ourselves, because we often want grace and understanding.

There is but little light in us and this we quickly lose through negligence.

Many times also we perceive not that we are so blind interiorly.

We often do ill and do worse in excusing it.

We are sometimes moved with passion, and we mistake it for zeal.

We blame little things in others and pass over great things in ourselves.

We are quick enough at perceiving and weighing what we suffer from others, but we mind not what others suffer from us.

He that would well and duly weigh his own deeds would have no room to judge hardly of others.

2. An internal man prefers the care of himself before all other cares, and he that diligently attends to himself is easily silent with regard to others.

Thou wilt never be internal and devout unless thou pass over in silence other men's concerns and particularly look to thyself.

If thou attend wholly to thyself and to God, thou wilt be little moved with what thou perceivest without thee.

Where art thou when thou art not present to thyself? And when thou hast run over all things, what profit will it be to thee if thou hast neglected thyself? (Matt. 16:26).

If thou desirest to have peace and true union thou must set all the rest aside and turn thine eyes upon thyself alone.

3. Thou wilt then make great progress if thou keep thyself free from all temporal care.

But if thou set a value upon anything temporal thou wilt fail exceedingly.

Let nothing be great in thine eyes, nothing high, nothing pleasant, nothing agreeable to thee, except it be purely God or of God.

Look upon all the comfort which thou meetest with from any creature as vain.

A soul that loveth God despiseth all things that are less than God.

None but God, eternal and incomprehensible, who filleth all things, can afford true comfort to the soul and true joy to the heart.

CHAPTER VI

Joy of a Good Conscience

THE glory of a good man is the testimony of a good conscience. (2 Cor. 1:12).

Keep a good conscience and thou shalt always have joy.

A good conscience can bear very much and is very joyful in the midst of adversity.

A bad conscience is always fearful and uneasy.

Sweetly wilt thou take thy rest if thy heart reprehend thee not. (Prov. 3:24).

Never rejoice but when thou hast done well.

The wicked never have true joy, neither do they feel internal peace, because "There is no peace to the wicked, saith the Lord." (Is. 48:22).

And if they shall say: We are in peace, evils will not come upon us, and who shall dare to hurt us? believe them not, for the wrath of God will rise on a sudden, and their deeds shall be brought to nothing, and their projects shall perish.

2. To glory in tribulation is not hard to him that loves, for so to glory is to glory in the Cross of Our Lord. (Gal. 6:14).

That glory is short-lived which is given and taken by men.

The glory of this world is always accompanied with sorrow.

The glory of good men is in their own consciences, not in the mouths of men.

The joy of the just is from God and in God, and they rejoice in the truth. (1 Cor. 13:6).

He that desires true and everlasting glory values not that which is temporal.

And he that seeks after temporal glory or does not heartily despise it, shows himself to have but little love for that which is heavenly.

That man has great tranquillity of heart who neither cares for praises nor dispraises.

3. He will easily be content and in peace whose conscience is clean.

Thou art not more holy if thou art praised nor anything the worse if thou art dispraised.

What thou art that thou art, nor canst thou be said to be greater than God sees thee to be.

If thou consider well what thou art within thyself thou wilt not care what men say of thee.

Man beholds the face, but God looks upon the heart. Man considers the actions, but God weighs the intentions.

To do always well and to hold one's self in small account is a mark of an humble soul.

To refuse comfort from any created thing is a sign of great purity and interior confidence.

4. He that seeks no outward testimony for himself shows

plainly that he has committed himself wholly to God.

"For not he who commendeth himself," saith St. Paul, "is approved, but he whom God commendeth." (2 Cor. 10:18).

To walk with God within and not to be held by any affection without, is the state of an internal man.

CHAPTER VII
Love of Jesus

B LESSED is he who knows what it is to love Jesus and to despise himself for the sake of Jesus.

We must quit what we love for this Beloved, because Jesus will be loved alone above all things.

The love of things created is deceitful and inconstant.

The love of Jesus is faithful and enduring.

He that cleaveth to creatures shall fall with them.

He that embraceth Jesus shall stand firm forever.

Love Him and keep Him for thy friend, who, when all go away, will not leave thee nor suffer thee to perish in the end.

Thou must at last be separated from all things else, whether thou wilt or not.

2. Keep thyself with Jesus both in life and death and commit thyself to His care, who alone can help thee when all others fail.

Thy Beloved is of such a nature that He will admit of no other, but will have thy heart to Himself, and sit there like a king upon his own throne.

If thou couldst but purge thyself well from affection to creatures, Jesus would willingly dwell with thee.

Thou wilt find all that in a manner lost, which thou hast placed in men out of Jesus.

Do not trust or rely upon a frail reed; "for all flesh is grass

and all the glory thereof shall fade as the flower of the field."
(Is. 40:6).

3. Thou wilt soon be deceived if thou only regard the outward show of men.

For if thou seek thy comfort and thy gain in others, thou wilt often meet with loss.

If in all things thou seek Jesus, doubtless thou wilt find Jesus.

But if thou seek thyself thou wilt indeed find thyself, to thine own ruin.

For a man does himself more harm if he seek not Jesus, than the whole world and all his enemies could do him.

CHAPTER VIII

Of Friendship with Jesus

WHEN Jesus is present all things go well, and nothing seems difficult; but when Jesus is absent everything is hard.

When Jesus speaks not within, our comfort is worthless; but if Jesus speak but one word, we feel great consolation.

Did not Mary Magdalen immediately arise from the place where she wept when Martha said to her, "The Master is here, and calleth for thee"? (John 11:28).

Happy hour, when Jesus calls from tears to joy of spirit!

How hard and dry art thou without Jesus! How foolish and vain if thou desire anything out of Jesus! Is not this a greater loss than if thou wert to lose the whole world? (Luke 9:25).

2. What can the world profit thee without Jesus?

To be without Jesus is a grievous hell and to be with Jesus a sweet paradise.

If Jesus be with thee no enemy can hurt thee. (Rom. 8:31).

Whosoever finds Jesus finds a good treasure, yea, good above all goods.

And he that loses Jesus loseth exceeding much, and more than if he lost the whole world.

He is wretchedly poor who lives without Jesus, and he is exceedingly rich who is well with Jesus.

3. It is a great art to know how to converse with Jesus, and to know how to keep Jesus is great wisdom.

Be humble and peaceable, and Jesus will be with thee.

Be devout and quiet, and Jesus will stay with thee.

Thou mayest quickly drive away Jesus and lose His grace if thou dost decline after outward things.

And if thou drive Him away from thee and lose Him, to whom wilt thou fly, and whom then wilt thou seek for thy friend?

Without a friend thou canst not well live, and if Jesus be not thy friend above all, thou wilt be exceedingly sad and desolate.

Thou actest then foolishly if thou put thy trust or rejoice in any other.

We ought rather choose to have the whole world against us than to offend Jesus.

Of all, therefore, that are dear to thee, let Jesus always be thy special beloved.

4. Let all things be loved for Jesus' sake, but Jesus for His own sake.

Jesus Christ alone is singularly to be loved, who alone is found good and faithful above all friends.

For His sake, and in Him, let both friends and enemies be dear to thee, and for all these thou must pray to Him that all may know and love Him.

Neither desire to be singularly praised nor beloved; for this belongs to God alone, who hath none like to Himself.

Neither desire that anyone's heart should be set on thee; nor do thou let thyself be taken up with the love of anyone, but let Jesus be in thee, and in every good man.

5. Be pure and free interiorly, without being entangled by any creature.

Thou must be naked and carry a pure heart to God, if thou wilt attend at leisure, and see how sweet is the Lord. (Ps. 33:9).

And, indeed, thou wilt never attain to this, unless thou be prevented and drawn by His grace, that so thou mayest all alone be united to Him alone, having cast out and dismissed all others.

For when the grace of God cometh to a man then he is strong and powerful for all things; and when it departs then he is poor and weak, left as it were only to stripes.

In these he must not be dejected nor despair, but stand with an even mind, resigned to the will of God, and bear, for the glory of Jesus Christ, whatever shall befall him; because after winter comes summer, after the night the day returns, after a storm there follows a great calm.

CHAPTER IX

Want of All Comfort

IT is not hard to despise all human comfort when we have divine.

But it is much, and very much, to be able to want all comfort, both human and divine; and to be willing to bear this interior banishment for God's honour, and to seek one's self in nothing nor to think of one's own merit.

What great thing is it if thou be cheerful and devout when grace comes! This hour is desirable to all.

He rides at ease that is carried by the grace of God.

And what wonder if he feel no weight who is carried by the Almighty, and led on by the Sovereign Guide?

2. We willingly would have something to comfort us, and it is with difficulty that a man can put off himself.

The holy martyr Lawrence overcame the world with his Prelate, because he despised whatever seemed delightful in this world, and for the love of Christ he unrepiningly suffered the high priest of God, Sixtus, whom he exceedingly loved, to be taken away from him.

He overcame, therefore, the love of man by the love of the Creator; and instead of the comfort he had in man he made choice rather of God's pleasure.

So do thou also learn to part with a necessary and beloved friend for the love of God.

And take it not to heart when thou art forsaken by a friend; knowing that one time or other we must all part.

3. A man must go through a long and great conflict in himself before he can learn fully to overcome himself, and to draw his whole affection towards God.

When a man stands upon himself he is easily drawn aside after human comforts.

But a true lover of Christ, and a diligent pursuer of virtue, does not hunt after comforts, nor seek such sensible sweetnesses, but is rather willing to bear strong trials and hard labours for Christ.

Therefore, when God gives spiritual comfort, receive it with thanksgiving, but know that it is the bounty of God, not thy merit.

4. Be not puffed up, be not overjoyed, nor vainly presume, but rather be the more humble for this gift and the more cautious and fearful in all thine actions; for this hour will pass away and temptation will follow.

When comfort shall be taken away from thee, do not presently despair; but wait with humility and patience for the heavenly visit, for God is able to restore thee a greater consolation.

This is no new thing, nor strange to those who have experienced the ways of God: for the great saints and ancient prophets have often felt this kind of variety.

5. Hence one said, at the time when grace was with him: "In my abundance I said I shall never be moved." (Ps. 29:7).

But when grace was withdrawn he immediately tells us what he experienced in himself: "Thou turnedst away thy face from me and I became troubled." (Ps. 29:8).

Yet in the meantime he despairs not, but more earnestly prays to the Lord, and says: "To thee, O Lord, will I cry, and I will make supplication to my God." (Ps. 29:9).

At length he receives the fruit of his prayer, and witnesseth that he was heard, saying, "The Lord hath heard me, and hath had mercy on me: The Lord became my helper." (Ps. 29:11).

But in what manner? "Thou hast turned for me," says he, "my mourning into joy, and thou hast compassed me with gladness." (Ps. 29:12).

If it has been thus with great saints, we that are weak and poor must not be discouraged if we are sometimes fervent, sometimes cold, because the Spirit comes and goes according to His own good pleasure. Wherefore holy Job says: "Thou visitest him early in the morning, and thou provest him suddenly." (Job 7:18).

6. Wherein then can I hope, or in what must I put my trust, but in God's great mercy alone, and in the hope of heavenly grace?

For whether I have with me good men, or devout brethren, or faithful friends, or holy books, or fine treatises, or sweet singing and hymns, all these help little, and give me but little relish, when I am forsaken by grace and left in my own poverty.

At such a time there is no better remedy than patience and self-denial under the will of God.

7. I never found anyone so religious and devout as not to have sometimes a subtraction of grace, or feel a diminution of fervour.

No saint was ever so highly rapt and illuminated as not to be tempted sooner or later.

For he is not worthy of the high contemplation of God who has not, for God's sake, been exercised with some tribulation.

For temptation going before is usually a sign of ensuing consolation.

For heavenly comfort is promised to such as have been proved by temptation. "To him that overcometh," saith Our Lord, "I will give to eat of the tree of life." (Apoc. 2:7).

8. Now divine consolation is given that a man may be better able to support adversities.

And temptation follows that he may not be proud of it.

The devil never sleeps, neither is the flesh yet dead: therefore thou must not cease to prepare thyself for battle, for on the right hand, and on the left, are enemies that never rest.

CHAPTER X

The Grace of God

WHY seekest thou rest, since thou art born to labour? Dispose thyself to patience rather than consolation, and to bear the Cross rather than to rejoice.

For who is there among worldly people that would not willingly receive comfort and spiritual joy, if he could always have it?

For spiritual consolation exceeds all the delights of the world and the pleasures of the flesh.

For all worldly delights are either vain or filthy; but spiritual delights alone are pleasant and honourable, springing from virtue, and infused by God into pure minds.

But these divine consolations no man can always enjoy when he will, because the time of temptation is not long absent.

2. But what very much opposes these heavenly visits is a false liberty of mind and a great confidence in one's self.

God doth well in giving the grace of consolation, but man doth ill in not returning it all to God with thanksgiving.

And this is the reason why the gifts of grace cannot flow in us, because we are ungrateful to the Giver, nor do we return all to the Fountainhead.

For grace will always be given to him that duly returns thanks, and what is wont to be given to the humble will be taken away from the proud.

3. I would not have any such consolation as would rob me of compunction, nor do I wish to have any such contemplation as leads to pride.

For all that is high is not holy; nor all that is pleasant good; nor every desire pure; nor is everything that is dear to us pleasing to God.

I willingly accept of that grace which always makes me more humble and fearful, and more ready to forsake myself.

He that has been taught by the gift of grace, and been instructed by the scourge of its withdrawal, will not dare to attribute anything of good to himself, but rather acknowledge himself to be poor and naked.

Give to God what is His (Matt. 22:21), and take to thyself what is thine; that is, give thanks to God for His grace; but as to thyself, be sensible that nothing is to be attributed to thee but sin and the punishment due to sin.

4. Put thyself always in the lowest place, and the highest shall be given thee, for the highest stands not without the lowest. (Luke 14:10).

The saints that are highest in the sight of God are the least in their own eyes; and the more glorious they are the more humble they are in themselves.

Being full of the truth and heavenly glory they are not desirous of vainglory.

They that are grounded and established in God can by no means be proud.

And they that attribute to God whatsoever good they have received seek not glory from one another, but that glory which is from God alone (John 5:44); they desire above all things that God may be praised in themselves, and in all the saints, and to this they always tend.

5. Be grateful then for the least and thou shalt be worthy to receive greater things.

Let the least be to thee as something very great, and the most contemptible as a special favour.

If thou considerest the dignity of the Giver, no gift will seem to thee little which is given by so great a God.

Yea, though He give punishment and stripes, it ought to be acceptable; for whatever He suffers to befall us, He always does it for our salvation. (Dan. 3:28).

He that desires to retain the grace of God let him be thankful for grace when it is given, and patient when it is withdrawn: let him pray that it may return; let him be cautious and humble, lest he lose it.

CHAPTER XI
Lovers of the Cross

JESUS has now many lovers of His heavenly Kingdom but few that are willing to bear His Cross.

He has many that are desirous of comfort, but few of tribulation.

He finds many companions of His table, but few of His abstinence.

All desire to rejoice with Him, few are willing to suffer with Him.

Many follow Jesus to the breaking of bread, but few to the drinking of the chalice of His Passion.

Many reverence His miracles, but few follow the ignominy of His cross.

Many love Jesus as long as they meet with no adversity.

Many praise Him and bless Him as long as they receive consolation from Him.

But if Jesus hide Himself, and leave them for a little while, they either fall into complaints or excessive dejection.

2. But they that love Jesus for Jesus' sake and not for any comfort of their own, bless Him no less in tribulation and anguish of heart than in the greatest consolation.

And if He should never give them His comfort, yet would they always praise Him and always give Him thanks.

3. Oh, how much is the pure love of Jesus able to do when it is not mixed with any self- interest or self-love.

Are not all those to be called hirelings who are always seeking consolation?

Are they not proved to be rather lovers of themselves than of Christ who are always thinking of their own profit and gain?

Where shall we find a man that is willing to serve God gratis?

4. Seldom do we find anyone so spiritual as to be stripped of all things.

For who shall be able to find the man that is truly poor in spirit and stripped of all affection to all created things? His price is from afar and from the uttermost coasts. (Prov. 31:10).

If a man give his whole substance it is yet nothing. (1 Cor. 13:3).

And if he do great penance it is yet little.

And if he attain to all knowledge he is far off still.

And if we have great virtue and exceeding fervent devotion there is still much wanting to him, to wit, one thing which is chiefly necessary for him. (Luke 10:42).

And what is that? That, having left all things else, he leave also himself and wholly go out of himself and retain nothing of self-love.

And when he shall have done all things which he knows should be done, let him think that he has done nothing.

5. Let him not make great account of that which may appear much to be esteemed, but let him in truth acknowledge himself to be an unprofitable servant, as Truth itself has said: "When you shall have done all the things that are commanded you, say: We are unprofitable servants." (Luke 17:10).

Then may he be truly poor and naked in spirit and may say with the Prophet: "I am alone and poor." (Ps. 24:16).

Yet no one is indeed richer than such a man, none more powerful, none more free, who knows how to leave himself and all things and place himself in the very lowest place.

CHAPTER XII
Highway of the Cross

TO many this seems a hard saying: "Deny thyself, take up thy cross, and follow Jesus." (Matt. 16:24).

But it will be much harder to hear that last word: "Depart from me, ye cursed, into everlasting fire." (Matt. 25:41).

For they that at present willingly hear and follow the word of the cross shall not then be afraid of eternal condemnation.

This sign of the cross will be in Heaven when the Lord shall come to judge.

Then all the servants of the cross, who in their lifetime have conformed themselves to Him that was crucified, shall come to Christ their judge with great confidence.

2. Why then art thou afraid to take up thy cross, which leads to a kingdom?

In the cross is salvation; in the cross is life; in the cross is protection from thine enemies.

In the cross is infusion of heavenly sweetness; in the cross is strength of mind; in the cross is joy of spirit.

In the cross is the height of virtue; in the cross is the perfection of sanctity.

There is no health of the soul nor hope of eternal life but in the cross.

Take up, therefore, thy cross and follow Jesus, and thou shalt go into life everlasting.

He is gone before thee carrying His own Cross; and He died for thee upon the Cross that thou mayest also bear thy cross and love to die on the cross.

Because if thou die with Him thou shalt also live with Him, and if thou art His companion in suffering thou shalt also partake in His glory. (2 Cor. 1:7).

3. Behold the cross is all and in dying to thy self all consists, and there is no other way to life and to true internal peace but the holy way of the cross and of daily mortification.

Go where thou wilt, seek what thou wilt, and thou shalt not find a higher way above, nor a safer way below than the way of the holy cross.

Dispose and order all things according as thou wilt and as seems best to thee, and thou wilt still find something to suffer, either willingly or unwillingly, and so thou shalt still find the cross.

For either thou shalt feel pain in the body, or sustain in thy soul tribulation of spirit.

4. Sometimes thou shalt be left by God, other times thou shalt be afflicted by thy neighbour, and what is more, thou shalt often be a trouble to thyself.

Neither canst thou be delivered or eased by any remedy or comfort, but as long as it shall please God thou must bear it.

For God would have thee learn to suffer tribulation without comfort, and wholly to submit thyself to Him, and to become more humble by tribulation.

No man hath so lively a feeling of the Passion of Christ as he who hath happened to suffer suchlike things.

The cross, therefore, is always ready and everywhere waits for thee.

Thou canst not escape it, whithersoever thou runnest; for whithersoever thou goest thou carriest thyself with thee and shalt always find thyself.

Turn thyself upwards, or turn thyself downwards; turn thyself without, or turn thyself within thee, and everywhere thou shalt find the cross.

And everywhere thou must of necessity have patience if thou desirest inward peace and wouldst merit an eternal crown.

5. If thou carry the cross willingly, it will carry thee and

bring thee to thy desired end; to wit to that place where there will be an end of suffering, though here there will be no end.

If thou carry it unwillingly thou makest it a burden to thee and loadest thyself the more, and nevertheless thou must bear it.

If thou fling away one cross, without doubt thou shalt find another and perhaps a heavier.

6. Dost thou think to escape that which no mortal ever could avoid? What saint was there ever in the world without his cross and affliction?

Our Lord Jesus Christ Himself was not one hour of His life without suffering: "It behooved Christ to suffer," saith He, "and rise again from the dead, and so enter into his glory." (Luke 24:46).

And why dost thou pretend to seek another way than this royal way, which is the way of the holy cross?

7. The whole life of Christ was a cross and a martyrdom, and dost thou seek rest and joy?

Thou errest, thou errest, if thou seekest any other thing than to suffer tribulations; for this whole mortal life is full of miseries and beset on all sides with crosses.

And the higher a person is advanced in spirit the heavier crosses shall he often meet with, because the pain of his banishment increases in proportion to his love.

8. Yet this man, thus many ways afflicted, is not without some allay of comfort, because he is sensible of the great profit which he reaps by bearing the cross.

For whilst he willingly resigns himself to it, all the burden of tribulation is converted into an assured hope of comfort from God.

And the more the flesh is brought down by affliction the more the spirit is strengthened by inward grace.

And it sometimes gains such strength through affection to tribulation and adversity, by loving to be conformable to the Cross of Christ, as not to be willing to be without suffering and affliction; because it is confident that it is so much the more acceptable to God, as it shall be able to bear more and greater things for Him.

This is not man's power, but the grace of Christ, which can and does effect such great things in frail flesh, that what it naturally abhors and flies, even this, through fervour of spirit, it now embraces and loves.

9. To bear the cross, to love the cross, to chastise the body, and bring it under subjection; to fly honours, to be willing to suffer reproaches, to despise one's self and wish to be despised; to bear all adversities and losses, and to desire no prosperity in this world, are not according to man's natural inclination.

If thou look upon thyself, thou canst do nothing of this of thyself.

But if thou confide in the Lord, strength will be given thee from Heaven, and the world and the flesh shall be made subject to thee.

Neither shalt thou fear thine enemy, the devil, if thou be armed with faith and signed with the Cross of Christ.

10. Set thyself then like a good and faithful servant of Christ, to bear manfully the Cross of thy Lord, crucified for the love of thee.

Prepare thyself to suffer many adversities and divers evils in this miserable life; for so it will be with thee wherever thou art, and so indeed wilt thou find it wheresoever thou mayest hide thyself.

It must be so, and there is no remedy against the tribulation of evil and sorrow but to bear them patiently.

Drink of the chalice of thy Lord lovingly if thou desire to be His friend and to have part with Him. (Matt. 20:22).

Leave consolations to God, to do with them as best pleaseth Him.

But prepare thou thyself to bear tribulations, and account them the greatest consolations; for the sufferings of this life bear no proportion to the glory to come (Rom. 8:18), although thou alone couldst suffer them all.

11. When thou shalt arrive thus far, that tribulation becomes sweet and savoury to thee for the love of Christ, then think that it is well with thee, for thou hast found a paradise upon earth.

As long as suffering appear grievous to thee and thou seek to fly from it, so long will it be ill with thee, and the tribulation from which thou fliest will everywhere follow thee.

12. If thou set thyself to what thou oughtst, that is to suffer and die to thyself, it will quickly be better with thee and thou shalt find peace.

Although thou shouldst have been rapt up to the third heaven with St. Paul (2 Cor. 12:2), thou art not thereby assured that thou shalt suffer no adversity. "I" said Jesus, "will show him how great things he must suffer for my name." (Acts 9:16).

To suffer therefore, is what waits for thee, if thou wilt love Jesus and constantly serve Him.

13. Would to God thou wert worthy to suffer something for the name of Jesus! how great a glory would be laid up for thee, how great joy would it be to all the saints of God and how great edification to thy neighbour.

All recommend patience, but alas! how few there are that desire to suffer.

With good reason oughtst thou willingly to suffer a little for Christ, since many suffer greater things for the world.

14. Know for certain that thou must lead a dying life and the more a man dies to himself the more he begins to live to God.

No man is fit to comprehend heavenly things who has not resigned himself to suffer adversities for Christ.

Nothing is more acceptable to God, nothing more wholesome for thee in this world than to suffer willingly for Christ.

And if thou wert to choose, thou oughtest to wish rather to suffer adversities for Christ than to be delighted with many comforts, because thou wouldst thus be more like unto Christ and more conformable to all the saints.

For our merit and the advancement of our state consist, not in having many sweetnesses and consolations, but rather in bearing great afflictions and tribulations.

15. If, indeed, there had been anything better and more beneficial to man's salvation than suffering, Christ certainly would have showed it by word and example.

For He manfully exhorts both His disciples that followed Him and all that desire to follow Him to bear the cross, saying: "If any one will come after me, let him deny himself and take up his cross and follow me." (Luke 9:23).

So that when we have read and searched all let this be the final conclusion, that "Through many tribulations we must enter into the kingdom of God." (Acts 14:21).

BOOK III

OF INTERNAL CONSOLATION

CHAPTER I
Christ to a Faithful Soul

DISCIPLE

I WILL hear what the Lord God will speak in me. (Ps. 84:9).

Blessed is that soul which heareth the Lord speaking within her (Prov. 8:34), and from His mouth receiveth the word of comfort.

Blessed ears which receive the veins of the divine whisper and take no notice of the whisper of the world.

Blessed ears indeed, which hearken to truth itself teaching within and not to the voice which soundeth without.

Blessed eyes which are shut to outward things and attentive to the interior. (Matt. 13:16).

Blessed they who penetrate into internal things and endeavour to prepare themselves more and more by daily exercises to the attainment of heavenly secrets.

Blessed they who seek to be wholly intent on God, and who rid themselves of every worldly impediment.

Mind these things, O my soul, and shut the doors of thy sensuality, that thou mayest hear what the Lord thy God speaks within thee.

CHRIST

2. Thus saith thy Beloved, I am thy salvation, thy peace, and thy life. (Ps. 34:3).

Abide in Me and thou shalt find peace.

Let alone all transitory things and seek things eternal.

What are all temporal things but deceit? And what will all things created avail thee if thou be forsaken by thy Creator?

Cast off then all earthly things and make thyself agreeable

to thy Creator and faithful to Him, that so thou mayest attain to true happiness.

CHAPTER II

Christ Speaks within Us

DISCIPLE

SPEAK, Lord, for Thy servant heareth. (1 Kgs. 3:9).

"I am thy servant, give me understanding that I may know thy testimonies." (Ps. 118:125).

Incline my heart to the words of Thy mouth, let Thy speech distill as the dew. (Ps. 71:6).

Heretofore the children of Israel said to Moses, "Speak thou to us and we will hear, let not the Lord speak to us lest we die." (Ex. 20:19).

Not thus, O Lord, not thus do I pray, but rather with the Prophet Samuel I humbly and longingly entreat Thee, "Speak, Lord, for Thy servant heareth."

Let not Moses nor any of the Prophets speak to me, but speak Thou rather, O Lord God, Who art the inspirer and enlightener of all the prophets, for Thou alone without them canst perfectly instruct me, but they without Thee will avail me nothing.

2. They may indeed sound forth words, but they give not the spirit.

They speak well, but if Thou be silent they do not set the heart on fire.

They deliver the letter, but Thou disclosest the sense. They publish mysteries, but Thou explainest the meaning of the thing signified.

They declare the Commandments, but Thou enablest us to keep them.

They show the way, but Thou givest strength to walk in it.

They work only outwardly, but Thou instructest and enlightenest the heart.

They water exteriorly, but Thou givest the increase.

They cry out with words, but Thou givest understanding to the hearing.

3. Let not then Moses speak to me but Thou, O Lord my God, the eternal Truth, lest I die and prove fruitless if I be only outwardly admonished and not enkindled within.

Lest the word which I have heard and not fulfilled, which I have known and not loved, which I have believed and not observed, rise up in judgment against me.

Speak then, O Lord, for Thy servant heareth (7 Kgs. 3:9), for Thou hast the words of eternal life. (John 6:69).

Speak that it may be for me some comfort to my soul and for the amendment of my whole life and to Thy praise and glory and everlasting honour.

CHAPTER III

The Word of God

CHRIST

MY son, hear My words, words most sweet, exceeding all the learning of the philosophers and of the wise men of this world. My words are spirit and life (John 6:69), and not to be estimated by the sense of man. They are not intended to gratify a vain self-complacency, but are to be heard in silence and received with all humility and great affection.

DISCIPLE

2. And I said: "Blessed is the man whom thou shalt instruct, O Lord, and shalt teach him thy law, that thou mayst give

him rest from the evil days" (Ps. 93:12-13) and that he may not be desolate upon earth.

CHRIST

3. It is I who have taught the prophets from the beginning and even till now I cease not to speak to all, but many are deaf to My voice and hard.

The greater number listen more willingly to the world than to God, and more readily follow the desire of the flesh than the good will of God.

The world promises things temporal and of small value and is served with great eagerness; I promise things most excellent and everlasting and men's hearts are not moved.

Who is there that serves and obeys Me in all things with that great care with which the world and its lords are served? "Be thou ashamed, O Sidon," saith the sea. (Is. 23:4). And if thou ask why, hear the reason.

For a small living men run a great way, for eternal life many will scarce move a single foot from the ground.

An inconsiderable gain is sought after; for one penny sometimes men shamefully quarrel, they are not afraid to toil day and night for a trifle or some slight promise.

4. But, alas, for an unchangeable good, for an inestimable reward, for the highest honour and never-ending glory they are unwilling to take the least pains.

Be ashamed then thou slothful servant who art so apt to complain, seeing that they are more ready to labour for death than thou for life.

They rejoice more in running after vanity than thou in the pursuit of truth.

And indeed they are sometimes frustrated of their hopes, but My promise deceives no man nor sends away empty him that trusts in Me.

What I have promised I will give, what I have said I will make good, provided a man continue to the end faithful in My love.

I am the rewarder of all the good and the strong trier of all the devout.

5. Write My words in thy heart and think diligently on them, for they will be very necessary in the time of temptation.

What thou understandest not when thou readest thou shalt know in the day of visitation.

I am accustomed to visit My elect in two ways, that is by trial and by comfort.

And I read them daily two lessons, one to rebuke their vices, the other to exhort them to the increase of virtues.

He that hath My words and slighteth them, hath that which shall condemn him at the last day. (John 12:48).

A Prayer to Impose the Grace of Devotion

6. O Lord, my God, Thou art all my good, and who am I that I should dare speak to Thee?

I am Thy most poor servant and a wretched little worm, much more poor and contemptible than I can conceive or dare express.

Yet remember, O Lord, I am nothing, I have nothing can do nothing. (2 Cor. 12:11).

Thou alone art good, just and holy; Thou canst do all things; Thou givest all things; Thou fillest all things, leaving only the sinner empty.

Remember Thy tender mercies and fill my heart with Thy grace, Thou Who wilt not have Thy works to be empty.

7. How can I support myself in this wretched life, unless Thy mercy and grace strengthen me?

Turn not Thy face from me; delay not Thy visitation; withdraw not Thy comfort, lest my soul become as earth without water unto Thee, (Ps. 142:6).

O Lord, teach me to do Thy will (Ps. 142:10), teach me to converse worthily and humbly in Thy sight, for Thou art my Wisdom, Who knowest me in truth and didst know me before the world was made and before I was born in the world. (Ps. 138:16).

CHAPTER IV
Walking in God's Presence

CHRIST

SON, walk before Me in truth and always seek Me in the simplicity of thy heart.

He that walks before Me in truth shall be secured from evil occurrences and truth shall deliver him from deceivers and from the detractions of the wicked.

If truth be on thy side thou wilt be free from all anxiety (John 8:32) and unconcerned at all that vain man can say against thee.

DISCIPLE

2. Lord, this is true; as Thou sayst so I beseech Thee, let it be done with me. Let Thy truth teach me, let Thy truth guard me and keep me till I come to a happy end. (Ps. 24:3). Let the same deliver me from all evil affections and all inordinate love and I shall walk with Thee in perfect freedom of heart.

CHRIST

3. I who am Truth will teach thee those things which are right and pleasing in My sight.

Think on thy sins with great compunction and sorrow and

never esteem thyself to be anything for thy good works.

Thou art indeed a sinner, subject to and entangled with many passions.

Of thyself thou always tendest to nothing, thou quickly fallest, thou art quickly overcome, easily disturbed and dissolved.

Thou has not anything in which thou canst glory, but many things for which thou oughtst to humble thyself, for thou art much weaker than thou art able to comprehend.

4. Let nothing then seem much to thee of all thou dost.

Let nothing appear great; nothing valuable or admirable; nothing worthy of esteem, nothing high, nothing truly praiseworthy or desirable, but what is eternal.

Let the eternal truth please thee above all things and thine own excessive vileness ever displease thee.

Fear nothing so much, blame and abhor nothing so much as thy vices and sins, which ought to displease thee more than any losses whatsoever.

Some persons walk not sincerely before Me; but being led with a certain curiosity and pride, desire to know the hidden things of My providence and to understand the high things of God, neglecting themselves and their own salvation.

These often fall into great temptations and sins through their pride and curiosity, because I stand against them.

5. Fear the judgments of God; dread the anger of the Almighty; but presume not to examine the works of the Most High, but search into thine own iniquities, how many ways thou hast offended and how much good thou hast neglected.

Some only carry their devotions in their books, some in pictures and some in outward signs and figures.

Some have Me in their mouths, but little in their hearts.

There are others, who, being enlightened in their understanding and purified in their affection, always breathe after things eternal, are unwilling to hear of earthly things and grieve to be subject to the necessities of nature, and such as these perceive what the spirit of truth speaks in them.

For it teaches them to despise the things of the earth and to love heavenly things; to disregard the world and all day and night to aspire after Heaven.

CHAPTER V
Effects of Divine Love

DISCIPLE

I BLESS Thee, O heavenly Father, Father of my Lord Jesus Christ; because Thou hast vouchsafed to be mindful of so poor a wretch as I am.

O Father of mercies and God of all comfort (2 Cor. 1:3), I give thanks to Thee, who sometimes art pleased to cherish with Thy consolation, me who am unworthy of any comfort.

I bless Thee and glorify Thee forevermore, together with Thine only-begotten Son and the Holy Ghost, the Comforter to all eternity.

O Lord God, my holy Lover, when Thou shalt come into my heart all that is within me will be filled with joy. (Prov. 23:5).

Thou art my Glory and the Joy of my heart.

Thou art my Hope and my Refuge in the day of my trouble. (Ps. 58:17).

2. But because I am as yet weak in love and imperfect in virtue, therefore do I stand in need of being strengthened and comforted by Thee. For this reason visit me often and instruct me in Thy holy discipline.

Free me from evil passions and heal my heart of all disorderly affections, that being healed and well purified in my interior, I may become fit to love, courageous to suffer and constant to persevere.

3. Love is an excellent thing, a great good indeed, which alone maketh light all that is burdensome and equally bears all that is unequal.

For it carries a burden without being burdened and makes all that which is bitter sweet and savory.

The love of Jesus is noble and generous; it spurs us on to do great things and excites us to desire always that which is most perfect.

Love will tend upwards and is not to be detained by things beneath.

Love will be at liberty and free from all worldly affections, lest its interior sight be hindered, lest it suffer itself to be entangled with any temporal interest or cast down by losses.

Nothing is sweeter than love; nothing stronger, nothing higher, nothing more generous, nothing more pleasant, nothing fuller or better in Heaven or on earth; for love proceeds from God and cannot rest but in God above all things created.

4. The lover flies, runs and rejoices, he is free and not held.

He gives all for all and has all in all, because he rests in one sovereign good above all, from whom all good flows and proceeds.

He looks not at the gifts, but turns himself to the giver above all goods.

Love often knows no measure, but is inflamed above all measure.

Love feels no burden, values no labours, would willingly do more than it can; complains not of impossibility, because it conceives that it may and can do all things.

It is able therefore to do anything and it performs and

effects many things where he that loves not faints and lies down.

5. Love watches, and sleeping, slumbers not. When weary is not tired; when straitened is not constrained; when frighted is not disturbed, but like a lively flame and a torch all on fire it mounts upwards and securely passes through all opposition. Whosoever loveth knoweth the cry of this voice.

A loud cry in the ears of God is the ardent affection of the soul, which saith, O my God, my love, Thou art all mine and I am all Thine. (Cant. 2:16).

6. Give increase to my love, that I may learn to taste with the interior mouth of the heart how sweet it is to love and to swim and to be dissolved in love. (Ps. 33:9).

Let me be possessed by love, going above myself through excess of fervour and ecstasy.

Let me sing the canticle of love, let me follow Thee my Beloved on high, let my soul lose herself in Thy praises, rejoicing exceedingly in Thy love.

Let me love Thee more than myself and myself only for Thee, and all others in Thee, who truly love Thee as the law of love commands, which shines forth from Thee.

7. Love is swift, sincere, pious, pleasant, and delightful; strong, patient, faithful, prudent, long- suffering, courageous, and never seeking itself.

For where a man seeks himself there he falls from love.

Love is circumspect, humble, and upright, not soft, not light, not intent upon vain things; is sober, chaste, stable, quiet, and keeps a guard over all the senses.

Love is submissive and obedient to superiors, in its own eyes mean and contemptible, devout and thankful to God; always trusting and hoping in Him, even when it tastes not the relish of God's sweetness, for there is no living in love without some pain or sorrow.

8. Whosoever is not ready to suffer all things and to stand resigned to the will of his Beloved, is not worthy to be called a lover.

He that loveth must willingly embrace all that is hard and bitter, for the sake of his Beloved, and never suffer himself to be turned away from Him by any contrary occurrences whatsoever.

CHAPTER VI

Proof of a True Lover

CHRIST

MY son, thou art not as yet a valiant and prudent lover.

DISCIPLE

Why, O Lord?

CHRIST

Because thou fallest off from what thou hast begun, upon meeting with a little adversity and too greedily seekest after consolation.

A valiant lover stands his ground in temptations and yields not to the crafty persuasions of the enemy.

As he is pleased with Me in prosperity so I displease him not when I send adversity.

2. A prudent lover considers not so much the gift of the lover as the love of the giver.

He looks more at the good will than the value, and prizes his Beloved above all His gifts.

A generous lover rests not in the gift, but in Me above every gift.

All is not lost if sometimes thou hast not that sense of devotion towards Me or My saints which thou wouldst have.

That good and delightful affection, which thou sometimes perceivest, is the effect of present grace and a certain foretaste of thy heavenly country, but thou must not rely too much upon it, because it goes and comes.

But to fight against the evil motions of the mind which arise, and to despise the suggestions of the devil is a sign of virtue and of great merit.

3. Let not, therefore, strange fancies trouble thee, of what kind soever they be that are suggested to thee.

Keep thy resolution firm and thine intention upright towards God.

Neither is it an illusion that sometimes thou art rapt into an ecstasy and presently returnest to the accustomed weakness of thy heart.

For these thou rather sufferest against thy will than procurest, and as long as thou art displeased with them and dost resist them it is merit and not loss.

4. Know that the old enemy strives by all means to hinder thy desire after good and to divert thee from every devout exercise, namely from the veneration of the saints, from the pious meditation of My Passion, from the profitable remembrance of thy sins, from keeping a guard upon thine own heart and from a firm purpose of advancing in virtue.

He suggests to thee many evil thoughts that he may weary thee out, and frighten thee that he may withdraw thee from prayer and the reading of devout books.

He is displeased with humble confession, and if he could he would cause thee to omit Communion.

Give no credit to him, value him not, although he often lays his deceitful snares in thy way.

Charge him with it when he suggests wicked and unclean things and say to him:

Begone, unclean spirit; be ashamed, miserable wretch; thou art very filthy indeed to suggest such things as these to Me.

Depart from me, thou wicked imposter, thou shalt have no share in me, but my Jesus will be with me as a valiant warrior and thou shalt be confounded.

I would rather die and undergo any torment whatsoever than yield to thy suggestions.

Be silent, I will hear no more of thee, although thou so often strivest to be troublesome to me. "The Lord is my light and my salvation, whom shall I fear? The Lord is the protector of my life, of whom shall I be afraid?" (Ps. 26:1).

"If armies in camp should stand together against me, my heart shall not fear. The Lord is my helper and my Redeemer." (Ps. 69:6).

5. Fight like a good soldier, and if sometimes thou fallest through frailty rise up again with greater strength than before, confiding in My more abundant grace, but take great care thou yield not to any vain complacency and pride.

Through this many are led into error and sometimes fall into incurable blindness.

Let this fall of the proud, who foolishly rely on their own strength, serve thee for a warning and keep thee always humble.

CHAPTER VII

Grace and Humility

MY son, it is more profitable and more safe for thee to hide the grace of devotion and not to be elevated with it, not to speak much of it, not to consider it much, but rather to despise thyself the more and to be afraid of it, as given to one unworthy.

Thou must not depend too much on this affection which

may be quickly changed into the contrary.

When thou hast grace think with thyself how miserable and poor thou art wont to be when thou art without it.

Nor does the progress of a spiritual life consist so much in having the grace of consolation, as in bearing the want of it with humility, resignation, and patience, so as not to grow remiss in thine exercise of prayer at that time, nor to suffer thyself to omit any of thine accustomed good works.

But that thou willingly do what lies in thee, according to the best of thy ability and understanding, and take care not wholly to neglect thyself through the dryness or anxiety of mind which thou feelest.

2. For there are many who when things succeed not well with them presently grow impatient or slothful.

Now the way of man is not always in his own power (Jer. 10:23), but it belongs to God to give and to comfort when He will, and as much as He will, and to whom He will, and as it shall please Him and no more.

Some, wanting discretion, have ruined themselves upon occasion of the grace of devotion, because they were desirous of doing more than they could, not weighing well the measure of their own weakness, but following rather the inclinations of the heart than the dictates of reason.

And because they presumptuously undertook greater things than were pleasing to God, therefore they quickly lost His grace.

They became needy and were left in a wretched condition, who had built themselves a nest in Heaven to the end, that being thus humbled and impoverished they might learn not to trust to their own wings, but to hide themselves under Mine. (Ps. 90:4).

Those who are yet but novices and unexperienced in the way of the Lord, if they will not govern themselves by the counsel of discreet persons, will be easily deceived and over-thrown.

3. And if they will rather follow their own judgment than believe others who have more experience, their future is full of danger if they continue to refuse to lay down their own conceits.

They that are wise in their own eyes seldom humbly suffer themselves to be ruled by others. (Prov. 3:7; Rom. 11:25).

It is better to have little knowledge with humility and a weak understanding, than greater treasures of learning with self-conceit.

It is better for thee to have less than much, which may puff thee up with pride.

He is not so discreet as he ought to be who gives himself up wholly to joy, forgetting his former poverty and the chaste fear of God, which apprehends the loss of that grace which is offered.

Neither is he so virtuously wise who, in the time of adversity or any tribulation whatsoever, carries himself in a desponding way and conceives and reposes less confidence in Me than he ought.

Adversity.
Trust in God.

4. He who is too secure in time of peace will often be found too much dejected and fearful in time of war.

If thou couldst but always continue humble and little in thine own eyes and keep thy spirit in due order and subjection, thou wouldst not fall so easily into dangers and offences.

It is a good counsel that when thou hast conceived the spirit of fervour, thou shouldst meditate how it will be with thee when that light shall leave thee.

Which, when it shall happen, remember that the light may return again, which, for thine instruction and My glory I have withdrawn from thee for a time.

5. Such a trial is oftentimes more profitable than if thou

wert always to have prosperity according to thy will.

For a man's merits are not to be estimated by his having many visions or consolations, nor by his knowledge in scriptures, nor by his being placed in a more elevated station.

But by his being grounded in true humility and replenished with divine charity; by his seeking always purely and entirely the honour of God; by his esteeming himself as nothing and sincerely despising himself, and being better pleased to be despised and humbled by others than to be the object of their esteem.

CHAPTER VIII

Our Unworthiness

DISCIPLE

I WILL speak to my Lord, I who am but dust and ashes. (Gen. 18:27). If I think anything better of myself, behold Thou standest against me and my sins bear witness to the truth, and I cannot contradict it.

But if I humble myself and acknowledge my own nothingness, and cast away all manner of esteem of myself and (as I really am) account myself to be mere dust, Thy grace will be favourable to me and Thy light will draw nigh to my heart; and all self-esteem, how small soever, will be sunk in the depth of my own nothingness and there lose itself forever.

It is there Thou showest me to myself, what I am, what I have been and what I am to come to; for I am nothing and I knew it not. (Ps. 72:22).

If I am left to myself, behold I am nothing and all weakness; but if Thou shouldst graciously look upon me, I presently become strong and am filled with a new joy.

And it is very wonderful that I am so quickly raised up and

so graciously embraced by Thee; I, who by my own weight, am always sinking to the bottom.

2. It is Thy love that effects this, freely preventing me and assisting me in so many necessities, reserving me also from grievous dangers, and as I may truly say, delivering me from innumerable evils.

For by an evil loving of myself, I lost myself, and by seeking Thee alone and purely loving Thee, I found both myself and Thee, and by this love have more profoundly annihilated myself.

Because Thou, O most sweet Lord, art bountiful to me above all desert and above all I dare hope or ask for.

5. Blessed be Thou, O my God, for though I am unworthy of all good, yet Thy generosity and infinite goodness never ceaseth to do good, even to those who are ungrateful and that are turned away from Thee.

Oh, convert us unto Thee, that we may be thankful, humble, and devout; for Thou art our salvation, our power, and our strength. (Ps. 61:8).

CHAPTER IX

All Things to be Referred to God

CHRIST

MY son, I must be thy chief and last end if thou desirest to be truly happy.

By this intention shall thine affection be purified, which too often is irregularly bent upon thyself and things created.

For if in anything thou seek thy self thou presently faintest away within thyself and growest dry.

Refer, therefore, all things principally to Me, for it is I that have given thee all.

Consider everything as flowing from the Sovereign Good, and therefore they must all be returned to Me as to their origin.

2. Out of Me, both little and great, rich and poor, as out of a living fountain, draw living water. (Is. 12:3).

And they who freely and willingly serve Me shall receive grace for grace. (John 10:6).

But he that would glory in anything else besides me, or delight in any good as his own (not referred to Me), shall not be established in true joy, nor enlarged in his heart, but in many kinds shall meet with perplexities and anguish.

Therefore thou must not ascribe anything of good to thyself, nor attribute virtue to any man, but give all to God, without whom man is nothing. (Ps. 113:1).

I have given all, I will have all returned to Me again and I very strictly require thanks for all that I give. (Matt. 25:28).

3. This is that truth by which all vainglory is put to flight.

And if heavenly grace and true charity come in there shall be no envy or narrowness of heart, nor shall self-love keep its hold.

For divine charity overcomes all and dilates all the powers of the soul.

If thou art truly wise thou wilt rejoice in Me alone; thou wilt hope in Me alone, for none is good but God alone, who is to be praised above all and to be blessed in all. (Dan. 3:56).

CHAPTER X

The Service of God

DISCIPLE

NOW will I speak, O Lord, and will not be silent; I will say in the hearing of my God, my Lord and my King that is on high.

Oh, how great is the multitude of Thy sweetness, O Lord, which Thou hast hidden for them that fear Thee. (Ps. 30:20). But what art Thou to those that love Thee? what to those that serve Thee with their whole heart?

Unspeakable indeed in the sweetness of Thy contemplation, which Thou bestowest on those that love Thee.

In this most of all hast Thou shown me the sweetness of Thy love, that when I had no being Thou hast made me, and when I strayed far from Thee Thou hast brought me back again, that I might serve Thee, and Thou hast commanded me to love Thee.

2. O Fountain of everlasting love, what shall I say of Thee?

How can I ever forget Thee who hast vouchsafed to remember me, even after I was corrupted and lost?

Thou hast, beyond all hope, showed mercy to Thy servant, and beyond all my desert bestowed Thy grace and friendship upon me.

What returns shall I make to Thee for this favour? for it is a favour not granted to all to forsake all things and renounce the world and choose a monastic life.

Can it be much to serve Thee whom the whole creation is bound to serve?

It ought not to seem much to serve Thee, but this seems rather great and wonderful to me, that Thou vouchsafest to receive one so wretched and unworthy into Thy service and to associate him to Thy beloved servants.

3. Behold all things are Thine which I have and with which I serve Thee.

Although, on the contrary, Thou dost rather serve me than I Thee.

Lo! Heaven and earth, which Thou hast created for the service of man, are ready at Thy beck and daily do whatever Thou hast commanded them.

And this is yet but little, for Thou hast also appointed the angels for the service of man. (Heb. 1:14).

But what is above all this is that Thou Thyself hast vouchsafed to serve man and hast promised that Thou wilt give him Thyself.

4. What shall I give Thee for so many thousands of favours? Oh, that I could serve Thee all the days of my life!

Oh, that I were able, if it were but for one day, to serve Thee worthily!

Indeed Thou art worthy of all service, of all honour, and of eternal praise!

Thou art truly my Lord and I am Thy poor servant, who am bound with all my strength to serve Thee and ought never to grow weary of praising Thee.

This is my will, this is my desire, and whatever is wanting to me do Thou vouchsafe to supply.

5. It is a great honour, a great glory to serve Thee and to despise all things for Thee.

For they who willingly subject themselves to Thy most holy service shall have great grace.

They shall find the most sweet consolations of the Holy Ghost who, for the love of Thee, have cast away all carnal delights.

They shall gain great freedom of mind who, for Thy name, enter upon the narrow way and neglect all worldly care.

6. O pleasant and delightful service of God, which makes a man truly free and holy!

O sacred state of religious bondage, which makes men equal to angels, pleasing to God, terrible to the devils and commendable to all the faithful.

O service worthy to be embraced and always wished for, which leads to the supreme good and procures a joy that will never end.

CHAPTER XI
Moderation of Our Desires

CHRIST

SON, thou hast many things still to learn which thou hast not yet well learned.

DISCIPLE

2. What are these things, O Lord?

CHRIST

3. That thou conform in all things thy desires to My good pleasure, and that thou be not a lover of thyself, but earnestly zealous that My will be done.

Desires often inflame thee and violently hurry thee on, but consider whether it is for My honour or thine own interest that thou art most moved.

If thou hast no other view but Me thou wilt be well contented with whatever I shall ordain, but if there lurk in thee anything of self-seeking, behold, this it is that hinders thee and troubles thee.

4. Take care then not to rely too much upon any desire which thou hast conceived before thou hast consulted Me, lest afterwards thou repent or be displeased with that which before pleased thee and which thou zealously desirest as the best.

For every inclination which appears good is not presently to be followed nor every contrary affection at first sight to be rejected.

Even in good desires and inclinations it is expedient sometimes to use some restraint, lest by too much eagerness, thou incur distraction of mind; lest thou create scandal to others, by not keeping within discipline or even lest by the opposition which thou mayest meet with from others, thou be suddenly disturbed and fall.

5. In some cases thou must use violence and manfully resist the sensual appetite and not regard what the flesh has a mind for, or what it would fly from, but rather labour that, whether it will or not, it may become subject to the spirit.

And it must be chastised and kept under servitude, until it readily obeys in all things and learns to be content with a little and to be pleased with what is plain and ordinary, and not to murmur at any inconvenience.

CHAPTER XII

On Learning Patience

DISCIPLE

O LORD God, patience, as I perceive, is very necessary for me; for this life is exposed to many adversities.

For, notwithstanding all I can do to live in peace, my life cannot be without war and sorrow.

CHRIST

2. So it is, son; but I would not have thee seek for such a peace as to be without temptations or meet with no adversities.

But even then to think that thou has found peace, when thou shalt be exercised with divers tribulations and tried in many adversities.

If thou shalt say thou art not able to suffer so much, how then wilt thou endure the fire of Purgatory?

Of two evils one ought always to choose the less.

That thou mayest, therefore, escape the everlasting punishments to come labour to endure present evils with patience for God's sake.

Dost thou think the men of this world suffer little or nothing? Thou shalt not find it so, though thou seek out the most delicate.

But thou wilt say they have many delights and follow their own wills and, therefore, make small account of their tribulations.

Suppose it to be so, that they have all they desire, but how long dost thou think this will last?

Behold, like smoke they shall vanish away (Ps. 36:20), who abound in this world and there shall be no more remembrance of their past joys.

Nay, even whilst they are living they enjoy them not without a mixture of bitterness, irk-someness and fear.

For the very same thing in which they conceive a delight doth often bring upon them a punishment of sorrow.

It is but just it should be so with them that, since they inordinately seek and follow pleasures, they should not enjoy them without confusion and bitterness.

Oh, how short, how deceitful, how inordinate and filthy are all these pleasures!

Yet, through sottishness and blindness, men understand this not, but like brute beasts, for a small pleasure in this mortal life, they incur the eternal death of their souls.

But thou, my son, go not after thy lusts, but turn away from thine own will. (Ecclus. 18:30).

Delight in the Lord and He will give thee the requests of thy heart. (Ps. 36:4).

5. For if thou wilt be delighted in truth and receive more abundant consolation from Me, behold in the contempt of all worldly things and the renouncing of all those mean pleasures, thou shalt be blessed and an exceeding great comfort be derived to thy soul.

And the more thou withdrawest thyself from all comfort in

things created, the more sweet and the more powerful consolations wilt thou find in Me.

But thou shalt not at first attain to these without some sorrow and labour in the conflict.

The old custom will stand in thy way but by a better custom it shall be overcome.

The flesh will complain, but by the fervour of the spirit it shall be kept under.

The old serpent will tempt thee and give thee trouble, but by prayer he shall be put to flight; moreover, by keeping thyself always employed in useful labour his access to thee shall be in a great measure impeded.

CHAPTER XIII

On Obedience

CHRIST

SON, he who strives to withdraw himself from obedience withdraws himself from grace, and he that seeks to have things for his own particular use loses such as are common.

If a man doth not freely and willingly submit himself to his superior, it is a sign that his flesh is not, as yet, perfectly obedient to him, but oftentimes rebels and murmurs.

Learn then to submit thyself readily to thy superior if thou desire to subdue thine own flesh.

For the outward enemy is sooner overcome if the inward man be not laid waste.

There is no more troublesome or worse enemy to the soul than thou art thyself, when not agreeing well with the Spirit.

Thou must, in good earnest, conceive a true contempt of thyself if thou wilt prevail over flesh and blood.

Because thou hast yet too inordinate a love for thyself,

therefore art thou afraid to resign thyself wholly to the will of others.

2. But what great matter is it if thou, who art but dust and a mere nothing, submit thyself for God's sake to man, when I, the Almighty and the Most High, who created all things out of nothing, have for thy sake humbly subjected Myself to man?

I became the most humble and most abject of all, that thou mightest learn to overcome thy pride by My humility.

Learn, O dust, to obey; learn to humble thyself, thou that art but dirt and mire, and to cast thyself down under the feet of all men.

Learn to break thine own will and to yield thyself up to all subjection.

3. Conceive an indignation against thyself; suffer not the swelling of pride to live in thee, but make thyself so submissive and little, that all may trample on thee and tread thee under foot as the dirt of the streets.

What hast thou, vain man, to complain of?

What answer canst thou make, O wretched sinner, to those that reproach thee, thou that hast so often offended God and many times deserved Hell?

But Mine eye hath spared thee (1 Kgs. 24:11), because thy soul was precious in My sight, that thou mightest know My love and mightest be always thankful for My favour and that thou mightest give thyself continually to true subjection and humility, and bear with patience to be despised by all.

CHAPTER XIV
The Judgments of God

DISCIPLE

THOU thunderest forth over my head Thy judgments, O Lord, and Thou shakest all my bones with fear and trembling and my soul is terrified exceedingly. (Job 4:14).

I stand astonished and consider that the heavens are not pure in Thy sight. (Job 15:15).

If in the angels Thou hast found sin and hast not spared them, what will become of me?

Stars have fallen from Heaven and I that am but dust, how can I presume? (Apoc. 6:13).

They whose works seemed praiseworthy have fallen to the very lowest, and such as before fed upon the bread of angels I have seen delighted with the husks of swine. (Luke 15:16).

2. There is then no sanctity, if Thou, O Lord, withdraw Thy hand.

No wisdom avails if Thou cease to govern us.

No strength is of any help if Thou support us not.

No chastity is secure without Thy protection.

No guard that we can keep upon ourselves will profit us, if Thy holy providence watch not over us. (Ps. 126:1).

For if we are left to ourselves we sink and we perish; but if Thou visit us we are raised up and we live.

For we are unsettled, but by Thee we are strengthened; we are tepid, but by Thee we are inflamed.

3. Oh, how humble and lowly ought I to think of myself; how little ought I to esteem whatever good I may seem to have!

Oh, how low ought I to cast myself down under the bottomless depths of Thy judgments, O Lord, where I find myself to be nothing else but nothing, nothing!

O immense weight! O sea, that cannot be passed over, where I find nothing of myself but altogether nothing!

Where then can there be any reason for glorying in myself? where any confidence in any conceit of my own virtue?

All vainglory is swallowed up in the depth of Thy judgments over me.

4. What is all flesh in Thy sight? Shall the clay glory against Him that formed it? (Is. 45:9).

How can he be puffed up with the vain talk of men whose heart in truth is subjected to God?

The whole world will not move him whom truth hath established in humility. Neither will he be moved with the tongues of all that praise him who hath settled his whole hope in God.

For behold, they also that speak are all nothing, for they shall pass away with the sound of their words, but the truth of the Lord remaineth forever.

CHAPTER XV

Our Dispositions and Desires

CHRIST

MY son, say thus on every occasion: Lord, if it be pleasing to Thee let this be done in this manner.

Lord, if it be to Thine honour let this be done in Thy name.

Lord, if Thou see that this is expedient and approve it as profitable unto me, then grant that I may use it to Thine honour.

But if Thou know that it will be hurtful to me and not expedient for the salvation of my soul, take away from me such a desire.

For every desire is not from the Holy Ghost, though it seems to a man right and good.

And it is oftentimes hard to judge truly, whether it be a good or bad spirit that urges thee on to desire this or that; or whether thou art moved to it by thine own spirit.

Many in the end have been deceived, who at first seemed to be led by a good spirit.

2. Whatsoever, therefore, presents itself to thy mind as worthy to be desired, see that it be always with the fear of God and humility of heart that thou dost desire or ask for it, and above all, thou oughtest, with a resignation of thyself, to commit all to Me and to say:

Thou knowest, O Lord, what is best, let this or that be done as Thou wilt.

Give what Thou wilt, how much Thou wilt, and at what time Thou wilt.

Do with me as Thou knowest and best pleaseth Thee, and is most for Thine honour.

Put me where Thou wilt and do with me in all things according to Thy will.

I am in Thy hand, turn me round which way Thou wilt.

Lo, I am Thy servant (Ps. 118:125), ready to obey Thee in all things; for I do not desire to live for myself but for Thee; Oh, that I could do so, after a faithful and perfect manner!

PRAYER FOR THE FULFILLING OF THE WILL OF GOD

DISCIPLE

3. Grant me Thy grace most merciful Jesus, that it may be with me and may labour with me and continue with me to the end. (Wis. 9:10).

Grant me always to will and desire that which is most acceptable to Thee and which pleaseth Thee best.

Let Thy will be mine and let my will always follow Thine

and agree perfectly with it.

Let me always will or not will the same with Thee, and let me not be able to will or not will any otherwise than as Thou willest or willest not.

4. Grant that I may die to all things that are in the world, and for Thy sake love to be despised and not to be known in this world.

Grant that I may rest in Thee above all things desired and that my heart may be at peace in Thee.

Thou art the true peace of the heart, Thou art its only rest; out of Thee all things are hard and uneasy. In this peace, in the selfsame, that is in Thee, the one sovereign eternal good, I will sleep and I will rest. (Ps. 4:9). Amen.

CHAPTER XVI
Comfort is to be Sought in God

DISCIPLE

WHATSOEVER I can desire or imagine for my comfort, I look not for it in this life, but hereafter.

For if I alone should have all the comforts of this world, and might enjoy all its delights, it is certain they could not last long.

Wherefore, thou canst not, O my soul, be fully comforted, nor perfectly delighted but in God, the comforter of the poor and the support of the humble.

Expect a little while, my soul, wait for the divine promise, and thou wilt have plenty of all that is good in Heaven.

If thou desirest too inordinately these present things, thou wilt lose those that are heavenly and everlasting.

Let temporal things serve thine use, but the eternal be the object of thy desire.

Thou canst not be fully satisfied with any temporal good,

because thou wast not created for the enjoyment of such things.

2. Although thou shouldst have all created goods, yet this could not make thee happy and blessed; but in God, who created all things, thy beatitude and happiness consist.

Not such a happiness as is seen or extolled by the foolish admirers of this world, but such as good Christians look for, and of which they have sometimes a foretaste who are spiritual and clean of heart, whose conversation is in Heaven. (Phil 3:20).

All human comfort is vain and short.

Blessed and true is that comfort which is inwardly received from truth.

A devout man always carries about him Jesus, his comforter, and saith to Him: Be with me, O Lord Jesus, in all places and at all times.

Let this be my consolation, to be willing to want all human comfort.

And if Thy comfort also be withdrawn, let Thy will and just appointment for my trial be to me as the greatest of comforts.

"For thou wilt not be angry always, nor wilt thou threaten forever." (Ps. 102:9).

CHAPTER XVII

Casting our Care on God

CHRIST

SON, suffer Me to do with thee what I will; I know what is best for thee.

Thou thinkest as man; thou judgest in many things as human affection suggests.

Disciple

2. Lord, what Thou sayest is true; Thy care over me is greater than all the care I can take of myself.

For he stands at too great a hazard that does not cast his whole care on Thee. (1 Ptr. 5:7).

Lord, provided that my will remain but right and firm towards Thee, do with me whatsoever it shall please Thee.

For it cannot but be good whatever Thou shalt do by me.

If Thou wilt have me to be in darkness, be Thou blessed, and if Thou wilt have me to be in light, be Thou again blessed; if Thou vouchsafe to comfort me, be Thou blessed, and if it be Thy will I should be afflicted, be Thou always equally blessed.

Christ

3. Son, it is in this manner thou must stand affected if thou desire to walk with Me.

Thou must be as ready to suffer as to rejoice. Thou must be willing to be poor and needy as to be full and rich.

Disciple

4. Lord, I will suffer willingly for Thee whatsoever Thou art pleased should befall me.

I will receive with indifference from Thy hand good and evil, sweet and bitter, joy and sorrow, and will give Thee thanks for all that happens to me. (Job 2:10).

Keep me only from all sin and I will fear neither death nor Hell.

Cast me not off forever, nor blot me out of the Book of Life, and what tribulation soever befalleth me shall not hurt me. (Apoc. 3:5).

CHAPTER XVIII
The Example of Jesus Christ

CHRIST

SON, I came down from Heaven for thy salvation. I took upon Me thy miseries, not of necessity, but moved thereto by charity, that thou mightest learn patience and mightest bear without repining the miseries of this life.

For from the hour of My Incarnation till My expiring on the Cross, I was never without suffering.

I underwent a great want of temporal things; I frequently heard many complaints against Me; I meekly bore with confusions and reproaches; for My benefits I received ingratitude; for My miracles, blasphemies; and for My heavenly doctrine, reproaches.

DISCIPLE

2. Lord, because Thou wast patient in Thy lifetime, in thus chiefly fulfilling the commandment of Thy Father, it is fitting that I, a wretched sinner, should, according to Thy will, take all with patience and, as long as pleaseth Thee, support the burden of this corruptible life, in order to my salvation. (2 Mack. 6:25).

For though this present life be burdensome, yet it is now become, through Thy grace, very meritorious and, by the help of Thine example and the footsteps of Thy saints, more support able to the weak and more lightsome.

It is also much more consoling than it was formerly under the Old Law, when the gate of Heaven remained shut and the way to it seemed more obscure, when so few concerned themselves to seek the Kingdom of Heaven.

Neither could they, who were then just and to be saved,

enter into Thy heavenly Kingdom, before Thy Passion and the payment of our debt by Thy sacred death.

Oh, what great thanks am I obliged to return to Thee for having vouchsafed to show to me and to all the faithful a right and good way to an everlasting Kingdom.

For Thy life is our way, and by holy patience we walk on to Thee, Who art our crown. (John 14:6).

If Thou hadst not gone before and instructed us who would have cared to follow?

Alas, how many would have stayed afar off and a great way behind, if they had not before their eyes Thine excellent example?

Behold we are still tepid, notwithstanding all Thy miracles and the instructions we have heard: what then would it have been if we had not this great light to follow Thee.

CHAPTER XIX
On Supporting Injuries

CHRIST

WHAT is it thou sayest, My son? Cease to complain, considering My Passion and the sufferings of the saints.

Thou hast not yet resisted unto blood. (Heb. 12:4).

What thou sufferest is but little in comparison to them who have suffered so much; who have been so strongly tempted, so grievously afflicted, so many ways tried and exercised. (Heb. 11:33, 37).

Thou must then call to mind the heavy sufferings of others, that thou may the more easily bear the little things thou sufferest.

And if to thee they seem not little, take heed lest this also proceed from thine impatience.

But whether they be little or great strive to bear them with patience.

2. The better thou disposest thyself for suffering, the more wisely dost thou act, and the more dost thou merit: and thou wilt bear it more easily, thy mind being well prepared for it and accustomed to it.

Say not: I cannot take these things from such a man, and things of this kind are not to be suffered by me for he has done me a great injury, and he upbraids me with things I never thought of; but I will suffer willingly from another, and as far as I shall judge fitting for me to suffer.

Such a thought is foolish, which considers not the virtue of patience, nor by whom it shall be crowned, but rather weighs the persons and the offence committed.

3. He is not truly a patient man who will suffer no more than he thinks good and from whom it pleases him.

The truly patient man minds not by whom it is he is exercised, whether by his superior, or by one of his equals, or by an inferior: whether by a good and holy man, or by one that is perverse and unworthy.

But how much soever and how often soever any adversity happens to him from anything created, he takes it all with equality of mind, as from the hand of God, with thanksgiving and esteems it a great gain.

For nothing, how little soever, that is suffered for God's sake, can pass without merit in the sight of God.

4. Be thou therefore, ready prepared to fight if thou desirest to gain the victory.

Without fighting thou canst not obtain the crown of patience.

If thou wilt not suffer, thou refusest to be crowned; but if thou desirest to be crowned, fight manfully and endure patiently. (2 Tim. 2:5).

Without labour there is no coming to rest, nor without fighting can the victory be obtained.

DISCIPLE

5. May Thy grace, O Lord, make that possible to me which seems impossible to me by nature. (Luke 18:27).

Thou knowest that I can bear but little and that I am quickly cast down by a small adversity.

Let all exercises of tribulation become amiable and agreeable to me, for Thy name's sake; for to suffer and to be afflicted for Thee is very healthful to my soul.

CHAPTER XX

Our Infirmities and Miseries

DISCIPLE

I WILL confess against myself my injustice. (Ps. 21:5). I will confess to Thee, O Lord, my infirmity.

It is oftentimes a small thing which casts me down and troubles me.

I make a resolution to behave myself valiantly; but when a small temptation comes I am brought into great straits.

It is sometimes a very trifling thing from which proceeds a grievous temptation.

And when I think myself somewhat safe, I find myself sometimes, when I least apprehend it, almost overcome with a small blast.

2. Behold, then, O Lord, my abjection and frailty (Ps. 24:18), every way known to Thee.

Have pity on me and draw me out of the mire (Ps. 118:15), that I stick not fast therein, that I may not be utterly cast down forever.

This it is which often drives me back and confounds me

in Thy sight, to find that I am so subject to fall and have so little strength to resist my passions.

And although I do not altogether consent, yet their assaults are troublesome and grievous to me, and it is exceedingly irksome to live thus always in a conflict.

Hence my infirmity is made known to me, because wicked thoughts do always much more easily rush in upon me than they can be cast out again.

3. Oh, that Thou, the most mighty God of Israel, the zealous lover of faithful souls, wouldst behold the labour and sorrow of Thy servant, and stand by me in all my undertakings.

Strengthen me with heavenly fortitude, lest the old man, the miserable flesh, not fully subject to the spirit, prevail and get the upper hand, against which we must fight as long as we breathe in this most wretched life.

Alas! what kind of life is this, where afflictions and miseries are never wanting; where all things are full of snares and enemies.

For when one tribulation or temptation is gone another cometh: yea, and whilst the first still lasts, many others come on and these unexpected.

4. How can a life be loved that hath such great bitterness, that is subject to so many calamities and miseries.

How can it be called life since it begets so many deaths and plagues?

And yet it is loved and many seek their delight in it.

Many blame the world that it is deceitful and vain, yet they are not willing to quit it, because the concupiscence of the flesh overmuch prevails.

But there are some things that draw them to love the world—others to despise it.

The concupiscence of the flesh, the concupiscence of the

eyes, and the pride of life (John 2:16), draw to the love of the world; but the pains and miseries, which justly follow these things, breed a hatred and loathing of the world.

5. But alas! the pleasure of sin prevails over the worldly soul and under these briers she imagines there are delights (Job 30:7); because she has neither seen nor tasted the sweetness of God, nor the internal pleasures of virtue.

But they that perfectly despise the world and study to live to God under holy discipline, experience the divine sweetness that is promised for those who forsake all; and such clearly see how grievously the world is mistaken and how many ways it is imposed upon.

CHAPTER XXI

Resting in God

Disciple

ABOVE all things, and in all things, do thou, my soul, rest always in the Lord, for He is the eternal rest of the saints.

Give me, O most sweet and loving Jesus, to repose in Thee above all things created; above all health and beauty, above all glory and honour, above all power and dignity, above all knowledge and subtlety, above all riches and arts, above all joy and gladness, above all fame and praise, above all sweetness and consolation, above all hope and promise, above all merit and desire.

Above all the gifts and presents that Thou canst give and infuse, above all the joy and jubilation that the mind can contain and experience.

In fine, above angels and archangels, and all the hosts of Heaven, above all things visible and invisible, and above all that which is less than Thee, my God!

2. For Thou, O Lord, my God! art the best above all things. Thou alone most high; Thou alone most powerful; Thou alone most sufficient and most full; Thou alone most sweet and most comfortable.

Thou alone most beautiful and most loving; Thou alone most noble and most glorious above all things; in whom all things are found together in all their perfection, and always have been and always will be.

And, therefore, whatever Thou bestowest upon me, that is not Thyself, or whatever Thou revealest to me concerning Thyself, or promisest, as long as I see Thee not, nor fully enjoy Thee, is too little and insufficient.

Because, indeed, my heart cannot truly rest, nor be entirely contented, till it rest in Thee, and rise above all Thy gifts and all things created.

3. O my most beloved spouse, Christ Jesus, most pure lover, Lord of the whole creation, who will give me the wings of true liberty, to fly and repose in Thee? (Ps. 54:7).

Oh, when shall it be fully granted me to attend at leisure, and see how sweet Thou art, O Lord, my God? (Ps. 33:9).

When shall I fully recollect myself in Thee, that through the love of Thee I may not feel myself, but Thee alone, above all feeling and measure, in a manner not known to all?

But now I often sigh and bear my misfortune with grief.

Because I meet with many evils in this vale of miseries, which frequently disturb me, afflict me; and cast a cloud over me; often hinder and distract me, allure and entangle me, so that I cannot have free access to Thee, nor enjoy Thy sweet embraces, which are ever enjoyed by blessed spirits.

Let my sighs move Thee, and this manifold desolation under which I labour upon earth.

4. O Jesus! the brightness of eternal glory, the comfort of a soul in its pilgrimage, my tongue cannot express the senti-

ments of my heart, but my silence itself speaks to Thee.

How long doth my Lord delay to come?

Let Him come to me, His poor servant, and make me joyful; let Him stretch forth His hand, and deliver me, a wretch, from all anguish. (Ps. 137:7).

Oh, come, oh, come (Apoc. 22:20), for without Thee, I can never have one joyful day, nor hour, for Thou art my joy, and without Thee my table is empty.

I am miserable, and in a manner imprisoned, and loaded with fetters, till Thou comfort me with the light of Thy presence, and restore me to liberty and show me a favourable countenance.

5. Let others seek instead of Thee, whatever else pleases them; nothing else doth please me or shall please me, but Thou my God, my hope, my eternal salvation.

I will not hold my peace, nor cease to pray, till Thy grace returns and Thou speak to me interiorly.

CHRIST

6. Behold here I am, behold I come to thee, because thou hast called upon Me. Thy tears and the desire of thy soul, thy humiliation and contrition of heart have inclined and brought Me to thee. (Is. 38:5).

DISCIPLE

7. And I said, O Lord, I have called upon Thee and have desired to enjoy Thee, and am ready to renounce all things for Thee.

For Thou didst first stir me up that I might seek Thee.

Be Thou, therefore, blessed, O Lord; Who hast showed this goodness to Thy servant, according to the multitude of Thy mercies.

What hath Thy servant more to say in Thy presence, but to

humble himself exceedingly before Thee; always remembering his own iniquity and vileness.

For there is none like to Thee amongst all things that are wonderful in Heaven or on earth. (Ps. 85:8).

Thy works are exceedingly good, Thy judgments are true and by Thy providence all things are ruled.

Praise, therefore, and glory be to Thee, O Wisdom of the Father! let my tongue, my soul and all things created, join in praising and blessing Thee.

CHAPTER XXII
The Benefits of God

OPEN, O Lord, my heart in Thy law and teach me to walk in Thy Commandments. (2 Mach. 1:4).

Give me grace to understand Thy will, and to commemorate with great reverence and diligent consideration all Thy benefits, as well in general as in particular, that so I may be able worthily to give Thee thanks for them.

But I know and confess that I am not able to return Thee due thanks, not even for the least point.

I am less than any of Thy benefits bestowed upon me (Gen. 32:10); and when I consider Thine excellency, my spirit loses itself in the greatness of Thy majesty.

2. All that we have in soul and body, all that we possess outwardly, or inwardly, by nature or grace, are Thy benefits and commend Thy bounty, mercy, and goodness from whom we have received all good.

And though one has received more, another less, yet all is Thine, and without Thee even the least cannot be had.

He that has received greater things cannot glory in his own merit, nor extol himself above others, nor exult over the lesser; because he is indeed greater and better who attributes less to himself and is more humble and devout in returning thanks.

And he who esteems himself the vilest of men and judges himself the most unworthy, is fittest to receive the greatest blessings.

3. But he that has received fewer, must not be troubled, nor take it ill, nor envy him that is more enriched; but attend rather to Thee, and very much praise Thy goodness, that Thou bestowest Thy gifts so plentifully, so freely and willingly, without respect to persons. (Rom. 2:11).

All things are from Thee and therefore Thou art to be praised in all.

Thou knowest what is fit to be given to everyone; and why this person hath less and the other more, is not our business to decide, but Thine, who keepest an exact account of the merits of each one.

4. Wherefore, O Lord God, I take it for a great benefit not to have much, which outwardly and according to men might appear praiseworthy and glorious, so that a person considering his own poverty and meanness ought not, upon that account, to be weighed down or to be grieved and dejected, but rather to receive comfort and great pleasure.

Because Thou, O God, hast chosen the poor and humble, and those that are despised by this world, for Thy familiar friends and domestics. (1 Cor. 1:27).

Witness Thine Apostles themselves whom Thou didst appoint rulers over all the earth. (Ps. 44:17).

And yet they conversed in this world without complaint, so humble and simple, without any malice or guile, that they were even glad when they suffered affronts and reproaches for Thy name (Acts 5:41); and what the world flies from they embraced with great affection.

5. Nothing, therefore, ought to give such great joy to him

that loves Thee and knows Thy benefits, as the accomplishment of Thy will in himself and the pleasure of Thine eternal
appointment.

With which he ought to be so far contented and comforted
as to be as willing to be the least as anyone would wish to be
the greatest and to enjoy as much peace and content in the
lowest place (Luke 14:10) as in the highest, and to be as willing to be despicable and mean and of no name and repute
in the world as to be preferred in honour and greater than
others.

For Thy will and the love of Thine honour ought to be
regarded above all, and to comfort and please him more
than any benefits whatsoever, which he hath received or can
receive.

CHAPTER XXIII
Things which Bring Peace

CHRIST

SON, I will teach thee now the way of peace and
true liberty.

DISCIPLE

2. Do, Lord, as Thou sayest, for this is delightful for me to
hear.

CHRIST

3. Endeavour, My son, rather to do the will of another
than thine own.

Ever choose rather to have less than more.

Always seek the lowest place and to be inferior to everyone.

Always wish and pray that the will of God may be entirely
fulfilled in thee.

Behold such a man as this enters upon the coasts of peace and rest.

DISCIPLE

4. Lord, this Thy short speech contains much perfection.

It is short in words, but full in sense and plentiful in its fruit.

For if I could faithfully observe it I should not be so easily troubled.

For as often as I find myself disquieted and disturbed I am sensible it is because I have strayed from this doctrine.

But Thou, O Lord, who canst do all things, and always lovest the progress of the soul, increase in me Thy grace that I may accomplish these Thy words and perfect my salvation.

A PRAYER AGAINST EVIL THOUGHTS

5. O Lord my God, depart not far from me; O my God, have regard to help me (Ps. 70:12), for divers evil thoughts have risen up against me, and great fears afflict my soul.

How shall I pass without hurt? How shall I break through them?

CHRIST

6. I will go before thee, says He, and will humble the great ones of the earth. (Is. 45:2). I will open the gates of the prison and reveal to thee hidden secrets.

DISCIPLE

7. Do, Lord, as Thou sayst, and let all these wicked thoughts flee from before Thy face.

This is my hope and my only comfort: to fly to Thee in all tribulations, to confide in Thee, to call on Thee from my heart, and patiently to look for Thy consolations.

A Prayer for the Enlightening of the Mind

8. Enlighten me, O good Jesus, with the brightness of eternal light, and cast out all darkness from the dwelling of my heart.

Restrain my many wandering thoughts and suppress the temptations that violently assault me.

Fight strongly for me and overcome these wicked beasts (Lev. 26:6), I mean these alluring concupiscences, that peace may be made in Thy power (Ps. 121:7), and the abundance of Thy praise may resound in Thy holy court, which is a clean conscience.

Command the winds and storms; say to the sea, be thou still, and to the north wind, blow thou not, and a great calm shall ensue. (Matt. 8:26).

9. Send forth Thy light and Thy truth (Ps. 42:3), that they may shine upon the earth; for I am as earth that is empty and void (Gen. 1:2), till Thou enlighten me.

Pour forth Thy grace from above, water my heart with the dew of Heaven; send down the waters of devotion to wash the face of this earth, to bring forth good and perfect fruit.

Lift up my mind, oppressed with the load of sins, and raise my whole desires towards heavenly things, that, having tasted the sweetness of the happiness above, I may have no pleasure in thinking of the things of the earth.

10. Draw me away and deliver me from all unstable comfort of creatures; for no created thing can fully quiet and satisfy my desires.

Join me to Thyself by an inseparable bond of love; for Thou alone canst satisfy the lover, and without Thee all other things are frivolous.

CHAPTER XXIV

Curiosity

CHRIST

SON, be not curious and give not way to useless cares, (1 Tim. 1:4). What is this or that to thee? Do thou follow Me. (John 21:22).

For what is it to thee whether this man be such or such; or that man do or say this or the other.

Thou art not to answer for others, but must give an account for thyself; why, therefore, dost thou meddle with them?

Behold, I know every one and see all things that are done under the sun (Eccles. 1:14); and I know how it is with every one, what he thinks, what he would have and at what his intention aims.

All things, therefore, are to be committed to Me; but as for thy part, keep thyself in good peace and let the busybody be as busy as he will.

Whatsoever he shall do or say will come upon himself, because he cannot deceive Me.

2. Be not solicitous for the shadow of a great name; neither seek to be familiarly acquainted with many, nor to be particularly loved by men.

For these things beget distractions and great darkness in the heart.

I would willingly speak My words to thee and reveal My secrets to thee, if thou wouldst diligently observe My coming and open to Me the door of thy heart.

Be careful and watch in prayer and humble thyself in all things. (1 Ptr. 4:7).

CHAPTER XXV

Peace and Progress

CHRIST

SON, I have said, Peace I leave with you, My peace I give unto you; not as the world giveth do I give unto you. (John 14:27).

Peace is what all desire; but all care not for those things which appertain to true peace.

My peace is with the humble and meek of heart. Thy peace shall be in much patience.

If thou wilt hear Me and follow My voice thou shalt enjoy much peace.

DISCIPLE

2. What then shall I do, Lord?

CHRIST

3. In everything attend to thyself, what thou art doing and what thou art saying; and direct thy whole intention to this, that thou mayest please Me alone, and neither desire nor seek anything out of Me.

And as for the sayings or doings of others, judge of nothing rashly, neither busy thyself with things not committed to thy care, and thus may it be brought about that thou shalt be little or seldom disturbed.

But never to feel any trouble, nor to suffer any grief of heart or pain of body, is not the state of this present life, but of everlasting rest.

Think not, therefore, that thou hast found true peace if thou feel no burden; nor that then all is well if thou hast no adversary, nor that thou hast attained to perfection if all things be done according to thine inclination.

Neither do thou then conceive a great opinion of thyself, nor imagine thyself to be especially beloved, if thou experience great devotion and sweetness; for it is not in such things as these that a true lover of virtue is known, nor doth the progress and perfection of a man consist in these things.

Disciple

4. In what then, O Lord?

Christ

5. In offering thyself with thy whole heart to the will of God, not seeking the things that are thine, either in little or great, either in time or eternity.

So that with the same equal countenance thou mayest continue giving thanks, both in prosperity and adversity, weighing all things with an equal balance.

If thou come to be so valiant and long-suffering in hope, that when interior comfort is withdrawn thou canst prepare thy heart to suffer still more, and dost not justify thyself, as if thou oughtest not to suffer such great things.

But acknowledgest My justice in all thine appointments and praisest My holy name, then it is that thou walkest in the true and right way of peace and mayest hope, without any doubt, to see My face again with great joy. (Job 33:26).

And if thou arrive to an entire contempt of thyself, know then that thou shalt enjoy an abundance of peace, as much as is possible in this state of banishment.

CHAPTER XXVI
The Eminence of a Free Mind

DISCIPLE

LORD, this is the work of a perfect man, never to let one's mind slacken from attending to heavenly things and to pass through many cares, as it were without care, not like one torpid, but by a certain prerogative of a free mind, which does not cleave by an inordinate affection to anything created.

2. Preserve me, I beseech Thee, O my most merciful God, from the cares of this life (Luke 21:34), that I be not too much entangled by them; from the many necessities of the body, that I may not be ensnared by pleasure, and from all hindrances of the soul, lest being over come by troubles I be cast down.

I do not say from those things which worldly vanity covets with so much eagerness, but from those miseries, which, by the general curse of our mortality, as punishments weigh down and keep back the soul of Thy servant from being able, when it will, to enter into liberty of spirit.

3. O my God, who art unspeakable sweetness, turn unto bitterness for me all carnal comfort which withdraws me from the love of things eternal, and wickedly allures me to itself, by setting before me a certain present delightful good.

O my God, let not flesh and blood prevail over me (7 Cor. 15:50), let it not overcome me; let not the world and its transitory glory deceive me (1 John 2:17); let not the devil overreach me by his devices. (2 Cor. 2:11).

Give me fortitude that I may stand my ground; patience, that I may endure, and constancy, that I may persevere.

Give me, in lieu of all the comforts of this world, the most delightful unction of Thy spirit, and instead of carnal love, infuse into me the love of Thy name.

4. Behold! eating, drinking, clothing, and other necessaries appertaining to the support of the body, are burdensome to a fervent spirit. (Wis. 9:15).

Grant that I may use such things with moderation, and not be entangled with an inordinate affection to them.

It is not lawful to cast them all away, for nature must be supported; but to require superfluities and such things as are most delightful Thy holy law forbids; for otherwise the flesh would grow insolent against the spirit. (Gal. 5:17).

In all this I beseech Thee let Thy hand govern and direct me, that I may no way exceed.

CHAPTER XXVII
Self Love

CHRIST

MY son, thou must give all for all, and be nothing of thine own.

Know that the love of thyself is more hurtful to thee than anything in the world.

Everything, according to the love and inclination which thou hast to it, cleaveth to thee more or less.

If thy love be pure, simple, and well ordered, thou shalt not be a captive to anything. (Matt. 6:22).

Covet not that which thou mayest not have.

Seek not to have that which may curb or rob thee of thine inward liberty.

It is wonderful that thou wilt not from the very bottom of thy heart commit thyself wholly to Me with all things that thou canst desire or have.

2. Why dost thou pine away with vain grief? Why dost

thou suffer thyself to be overwhelmed with useless cares?

Be resigned to My good pleasure and thou shalt suffer no loss.

If thou seek this or that, or would be here or there, for the sake of thine own interest, or of thine own will, thou shalt never be at rest, nor free from solicitude, for in everything thou wilt find some defect, and in every place there will be someone that will cross thee.

3. It is not, therefore, the obtaining or multiplying things exteriorly that avails thee, but rather the despising of them and cutting them up by the root out of thy heart.

This I would not have thee to understand only with regard to money and riches, but also with regard to the ambition of honour and the desire of empty praise, all which things pass away with the world. (John 2:17).

The place avails little if the spirit of fervour be wanting; neither shall that peace stand long which is sought from abroad, if the state of thy heart want the true foundation; that is, if thou stand not in Me, thou mayest change, but not better thyself.

For when occasion happens, thou shalt find that which thou didst fly from and even more.

A Prayer For Cleansing the Heart and Obtaining Heavenly Wisdom

Disciple

4. Confirm me, O God, by the grace of Thy Holy Spirit.

Give me power to be strengthened in the inward man and to cast out of my heart all unprofitable care and trouble; let me not be drawn away with various desires of anything whatsoever, whether it be of little or great value; but teach me to look upon all things as passing away and myself as passing along with them.

For nothing is lasting under the sun, where all is vanity and affliction of spirit. (Eccles. 2:11). Oh, how wise is he who considers things in this manner!

5. Give me, O Lord, heavenly wisdom that I may learn above all things to seek Thee and to find Thee (Wis. 9:10); above all things to relish Thee, and to love Thee, and to understand all other things as they are, according to the order of Thy wisdom.

Grant that I may prudently decline him that flatters me and patiently bear with him that contradicts me.

For it is great wisdom not to be moved with every wind of words, nor to give ear to the wicked, flattering siren; for thus shall we go on securely in the way we have begun.

CHAPTER XXVIII
On Detraction

CHRIST

SON, take it not to heart if some people think ill of thee, and say of thee what thou art not willing to hear.

Thou oughtest to think worse of thyself and to believe that no one is weaker than thyself.

If thou walk interiorly thou wilt make small account of flying words.

It is no small prudence to be silent in the evil time, and to turn within to Me, and not to be disturbed with the judgment of men.

2. Let not thy peace be in the tongues of men, for whether they put a good or bad construction on what thou dost, thou art not for all that other than thou art. Where is true peace and true glory? Is it not in Me?

And he who covets not to please men, nor fears their displeasure, shall enjoy much peace. (Col. 3:22).

All disquiet of heart and distraction of the senses arise from inordinate love and vain fear.

CHAPTER XXIX
The Time of Tribulation

DISCIPLE

BLESSED, O Lord, be Thy name forever, who hast been pleased that this trial and tribulation should come upon me. (Dan. 3:26).

I cannot fly from it, but must of necessity fly to Thee that Thou mayest help me, and turn it to my good.

Lord, I am now in tribulation, and my heart is not at ease; but I am much afflicted with my present suffering.

And now, dear Father, what shall I say? I am taken, O Lord, in these straits: O save me from this hour. (John 12:27).

But for this reason I came unto this hour, that Thou mightest be glorified when I shall be exceedingly humbled and delivered by Thee.

May it please Thee, O Lord, to deliver me; for, poor wretch that I am, what can I do and whither shall I go without Thee? (Ps. 108:21).

Give me patience, O Lord, at this time also.

Help me, O my God, and I will not fear how much soever I may be oppressed.

2. And now, in the midst of these things, what shall I say? Lord, Thy will be done (Matt. 6:10), I have well deserved to be afflicted and troubled.

I must needs bear it, and would to God it may be with patience, till the storm pass over and it be better.

But Thine almighty hand is able to take away from me this temptation also, and to moderate its violence, lest I quite sink under it, as Thou hast often done heretofore for me, O my

God, my mercy! (Ps. 58:18).

And the more difficult this is to me, the easier to Thee is this change of the right hand of the Most High. (Ps. 76:11).

CHAPTER XXX
The Divine Assistance

CHRIST

SON, I am the Lord, who give strength in the day of trouble. (Nahum 1:7).

Come to Me when it is not well with thee.

This is that which most of all hinders heavenly comfort, that thou art slow in turning thyself to prayer.

For before thou earnestly prayest to Me thou seekest in the meantime many comforts and delightest thyself in outward things.

And hence it comes to pass that all things avail thee little till thou take notice that I am He that delivers those that trust in Me. Nor is there out of Me any powerful help, or profitable counsel, or lasting remedy.

But now having recovered spirit after the storm, grow thou strong again in the light of My tender mercies; for I am at hand to repair all, not only to the full, but even with abundance and above measure.

2. Is anything difficult to Me? or shall I be like one that promises and does not perform? (Jer. 32:27; Num. 23:19).

Where is thy faith? Stand firmly and with perseverance.

Have patience and be of good courage, comfort will come to thee in its proper season.

Wait for Me, wait, I will come and cure thee.

It is a temptation that troubles thee, and a vain fear that frightens thee.

What does that solicitude about future accidents bring

thee but only sorrow upon sorrow? "Sufficient for the day is the evil thereof." (Matt. 6:34).

It is a vain and unprofitable thing to conceive either grief or joy for future things, which perhaps will never happen.

3. But it is incident to man to be deluded with such imaginations; and a sign of a soul that is yet weak and to be easily drawn away by the suggestions of the enemy.

For he cares not whether it be with things true or false that he abuses and deceives thee, whether he overthrow thee with the love of things present or the fear of things to come.

"Let not, therefore, thy heart be troubled and let it not be afraid." (John 14:27).

Believe in Me and trust in My mercy.

When thou thinkest I am far from thee, I am often nearest to thee.

When thou judgest that almost all is lost, then oftentimes it is that thou art in the way of gaining the greatest merit.

All is not lost when anything falls out otherwise than thou wouldst have it.

Thou must not judge according to thy present feeling, nor give thyself up in such manner to any trouble, from whence soever it comes, nor take it so as if all hope were gone of being delivered out of it.

4. Think not thyself wholly forsaken, although for a time I have sent thee some tribulation, or withdrawn from thee the comfort which thou desirest; for this is the way to the Kingdom of Heaven.

And without doubt it is more expedient for thee, and for the rest of My servants, that thou be exercised by adversities than that thou shouldst have all things according to thine inclination.

I know thy secret thoughts; I know that it is very expedient for thy soul that thou shouldst sometimes be left without consolation, lest thou shouldst be puffed up with much success and shouldst take a complacence in thyself, imagining thyself to be what thou art not.

What I have given I can justly take away, and restore it again when I please.

5. When I give it, it is still Mine; when I take it away again I take not anything that is thine; for every good gift and every perfect gift is Mine. (James 1:17).

If I send thee affliction or any adversity, repine not, neither let thy heart be cast down.

I can quickly raise thee up again and turn all thy burden into joy.

Nevertheless, I am just and greatly to be praised when I deal thus with thee.

6. If thou think rightly and consider things in truth thou oughtst never to be so much dejected and troubled for any adversity, but rather to rejoice and give thanks.

Yea, even to account this as a special subject of joy, that afflicting thee with sorrows I spare thee not. (Job 6:10).

"As my Father hath loved me I also have loved you," said I to My beloved disciples (John 15:9), whom certainly I did not send to temporal joys, but to great conflicts; not to honours, but to contempt; not to idleness, but to labours; not to rest, but to "bring forth much fruit in patience." (Luke 8:13). Remember these words, O My son.

CHAPTER XXXI
Disregard of All Things Created

DISCIPLE

LORD, I stand much in need of a grace yet greater, if I must arrive so far, that it may not be in the power of any man, nor anything created, to hinder me.

For as long as anything holds me I cannot freely fly to Thee.

He was desirous to fly freely to Thee who said: "Who will give me wings like a dove, and I will fly and be at rest." (Ps. 54:7).

What can be more at rest than a simple eye that aims at nothing but God? And what can be more free than he who desires nothing upon earth?

A man ought, therefore, to pass and ascend above everything created, and perfectly to forsake himself, and in ecstasy of mind to stand and see that Thou, the Creator of all, infinitely transcendest all creatures.

And unless a man be at liberty from all things created, he cannot freely attend to things divine.

And this is the reason why there are found so few contemplative persons, because there are few that wholly wean themselves from transitory and created things.

2. For this a great grace is required, which may elevate the soul and carry her up above herself.

And unless a man be elevated in spirit, and set at liberty from all creatures, and wholly united to God, whatever he knows, and whatever he has, is of no great weight.

Long shall he be little and lie grovelling beneath, who esteems anything great but only the one immense, eternal good.

And whatsoever is not God is nothing, and ought to be accounted as nothing.

There is a great difference between the wisdom of an illuminated and devout man and the knowledge of a learned and studious scholar.

Far more noble is that learning which flows from above, from the divine influence, than that which with labour is acquired by the industry of man.

3. Many are found to desire contemplation, but they care not to practice those things which are required thereunto.

It is a great impediment that we so much regard signs and sensible things, and have but little of perfect mortification.

I know not what it is, by what spirit we are led, or what we pretend to, who seem to be called spiritual persons, that we take so much pains, and have a greater solicitude for transitory and mean things, and scarce ever have our senses fully recollected to think of our own interior.

4. Alas! after a slight recollection we presently wander out of ourselves again, neither do we weigh well our works by a strict examination.

We take no notice where our affections lie, nor do we lament the great want of purity in all we do.

For all flesh had corrupted its way (Gen. 6:12), and therefore the great flood ensued.

As, therefore, our interior affection is much corrupted it must needs be that the action which follows should also be corrupted, which is the testimony of the want of inward vigour.

From a pure heart proceeds the fruit of a good life. (1 Tim. 1:3).

5. We are apt to inquire how much a man has done, but with how much virtue he has done it is not so diligently considered.

We ask whether he be strong, rich, beautiful, talented, a good writer, a good singer, or a good workman; but how poor he is in spirit, how patient and meek, how devout and internal, is what few speak of.

Nature looks upon the outward things of a man, but grace turns herself to the interior.

Nature is often deceived, but grace hath her trust in God that she may not be deceived.

CHAPTER XXXII
Renouncing Cupidity

Christ

SON, thou canst not possess perfect liberty un-less thou wholly deny thyself. (Matt. 16:24).

All self-seekers and self-lovers are bound in fetters full of desires, full of cares, unsettled, and seeking always their own ease, and not the things of Jesus Christ (Phil. 3:21), but oftentimes devising and framing that which will not stand.

For all shall come to nothing that proceeds not from God.

Take this short and perfect word: Forsake all and thou shalt find all, leave thy desires and thou shalt find rest. (Matt. 11:29).

Consider this well, and when thou shalt put it in practice thou shalt understand all things.

Disciple

2. Lord, this is no one day's work, no child's play; yea, in this short sentence is included the whole perfection of a religious man.

Christ

3. Son, thou must not be turned back, nor presently cast down, when thou hearest what the way of the perfect is: but rather be incited thereby to undertake great things, or at least to sigh after them with an earnest desire.

I would it were so with thee, and that thou wert come so far that thou wert no longer a lover of thyself, but didst stand wholly at My beck, and at his whom I have appointed father over thee; then wouldst thou exceedingly please Me, and all thy life would pass in joy and peace.

Thou hast yet many things to forsake, which, unless thou give up to Me without reserve, thou wilt not attain to that which thou demandest.

I counsel thee to buy of Me gold firetried, that thou mayest be made rich (Apoc. 3:18); that is, heavenly wisdom, which treads underfoot all things below.

Set aside the wisdom of the earth, that is, all seeking to please the world and thyself.

4. I have said that thou shouldst give the things that are high and of great esteem with men to purchase those which are esteemed contemptible.

For true heavenly wisdom seems very mean and contemptible, and is scarcely thought of by men; that wisdom, which teaches to think meanly of one's self, and not to seek to become great upon earth; which many praise in words, but in their life are far from it; yet this same is that precious pearl (Matt. 13:46), which is hidden from many.

CHAPTER XXXIII
Inconstancy of Our Heart

CHRIST

SON, trust not to thy present affection, it will quickly be changed into another.

As long as thou livest thou art subject to change, even against thy will; so as to be sometimes joyful, at other times sad; now easy, again troubled; at one time devout, at another dry; sometimes fervent, at other times sluggish; one day heavy, another lighter.

But he that is wise and well instructed in spirit, stands above all these changes; not minding what he feels in himself, nor on what side the wind of mutability blows; but that the whole bent of his soul may advance towards his due and wished-for end.

For so he may continue one and the selfsame, without being shaken, by directing without ceasing, through all this variety of events, the single eye of his intention towards Me. (Matt. 6:22).

2. And by how much purer the eye of the intention is, with so much greater constancy mayest thou pass through these divers storms.

But in many the eye of pure intention is dark, for men quickly look towards something delightful which comes in their way.

And it is rare to find one wholly free from all blemish of self-seeking.

So the Jews heretofore came into Bethania, to Martha and Mary, not for Jesus only, but that they might see Lazarus also. (John 12:9).

The eye of the intention therefore must be purified that it may be single and right, and must be directed unto Me, beyond all the various objects that interpose themselves.

CHAPTER XXXIV

The Love of God

DISCIPLE

BEHOLD, "my God, and my all!" What would I have more and what can I desire more happy.

O sweet and savoury word! but to him that loves the word, not the world, nor the things that are in the world. (1 John 2:15).

My God and my All! Enough is said to him that understands; and it is delightful to him that loves to repeat it often.

For when Thou art present all things yield delight; but when Thou art absent all things are loathsome.

Thou givest tranquillity to the heart, and great peace and pleasant joy.

Thou makest us to think well of all and praise Thee in all things; nor can anything without Thee afford any lasting pleasure; but to make it agreeable and relishing, Thy grace must be present, and it must be seasoned with the seasoning of Thy wisdom.

2. What can be distasteful to him who has no satisfaction but in Thee? and what can yield any true delight to him who relishes not Thee?

But the wise of this world and the admirers of the flesh are mistaken in their wisdom; because in the world is much vanity, and following the flesh leads to death. (Rom. 8:6).

But they that follow Thee by despising the things of this world, and mortifying the flesh, are found to be wise indeed, for they are translated from vanity to truth, from the flesh to the spirit.

Such as these have a relish of God, and what good soever is found in creatures they refer to the praise of their Maker.

But great, yea very great, is the difference between the relish of the Creator and the creature, of eternity and of time, of light uncreated and of light enlightened.

3. O Light eternal! transcending all created lights, dart forth Thy light from above, which may penetrate the most inward parts of my heart.

Cleanse, gladden, enlighten, and quicken my spirit with its powers, that I may be absorbed in Thee with ecstasies of joy.

Oh, when will this blessed and desirable hour come when Thou shalt fill me with Thy presence and become to me all in all. (1 Cor. 15:28).

As long as this is not granted to me my joy will not be full.

Alas! the old man is still living in me; he is not wholly crucified; he is not perfectly dead. (Rom. 6:6).

He still lusts strongly against the spirit; he wages war within me, and suffers not the kingdom of my soul to be quiet. (Gal. 5:17).

4. But, O Lord, who "rulest the power of the sea and appeasest the motion of the waves thereof" (Ps. 88:10), "arise and help me." (Ps. 43:26).

"Scatter thou the nations that delight in wars." (Ps. 67:31). Crush them by Thy power.

Show forth, I beseech Thee, Thy wonderful works (Ecclus. 17:7), and let Thy right hand be glorified (Ps. 88:14); for there is no hope nor refuge for me but in Thee, O Lord, my God.

CHAPTER XXXV

Insecurity Against Temptation

CHRIST

SON, thou art never secure in this life; but as long as thou livest thou hast always need of spiritual arms.

Thou art in the midst of enemies, and art assaulted on the right hand and on the left.

If then thou dost not make use of the buckler of patience on all sides thou wilt not be long without a wound.

Moreover, if thou dost not fix thy heart on Me with a sincere will of suffering all things for My sake thou canst not support the heat of this warfare, nor attain to the victory of the saints.

It behooveth thee, therefore, to go through all manfully, and to use a strong hand against all things that oppose thee.

For to him that overcometh is given manna (Apoc. 2:17), and to the sluggard is left much misery.

2. If thou seek rest in this life how then wilt thou come to rest everlasting?

Set not thyself to seek for much rest, but for much patience.

Seek true peace, not upon earth, but in Heaven; not in men, nor in other things created, but in God alone. (John 14:27).

Thou must be willing, for the love of God, to suffer all things, to wit: labours and sorrows, temptations and vexations, anxieties, necessities, sickness, injuries, detractions, reprehensions, humiliations, confusions, corrections, and contempts (James 1:2).

These things help to obtain virtue; these try a novice of Christ; these procure a heavenly crown.

I will give an everlasting reward for this short labour, and glory without end for transitory confusion.

Dost thou think to have always spiritual consolations when thou pleasest?

My saints had not these always; but met with many troubles, and various temptations and great desolations.

But they bore all with patience, and confided more in God than in themselves; knowing that the sufferings of this life bear no proportion to the greatness of the glory to come. (Rom. 8:18).

Wouldst thou have that immediately which others after many tears and great labours have hardly obtained.

"Expect the Lord, do manfully and let thy heart take courage" (Ps. 26:14); do not despond, do not fall off, but constantly offer both soul and body for the glory of God.

I will reward thee most abundantly, and will be with thee in all thy tribulation. (Ps. 91:15).

CHAPTER XXXVI
Vain Judgments

CHRIST

SON, cast thy heart firmly on the Lord, and fear not the judgment of man when thy conscience gives testimony of thy piety and innocence.

It is good and happy to suffer in this manner, neither will this be grievous to an humble heart, nor to him that trusts in God more than in himself.

Many say many things, and therefore little credit is to be given to them.

Neither is it possible to satisfy all.

Though Paul endeavoured to please all in the Lord and made himself all unto all (1 Cor. 9:22), yet he made little account of his being judged by the judgment of men. (1 Cor. 4:3).

2. He laboured for the edification and salvation of others as much as he could and as lay in him, but he could not prevent his being some times judged or despised by others.

Therefore he committed all to God, who knows all, and defended himself, by patience and humility, against the tongues of those that spoke evil, or that thought and gave out at pleasure vain and faulty things of him.

However, he answered them sometimes, lest his silence might give occasion of scandal to the weak.

3. "Who art thou, that thou shouldst be afraid of a mortal man?" (Is. 51:12). Today he is, and tomorrow he appears no more. (1 Mach. 2:63).

Fear God, and thou shalt have no need of being afraid of man.

What can anyone do against thee by his words or injuries? He rather hurts himself than thee, nor can he escape the judgment of God whoever he be. (2 Mach. 7:35).

See thou have God before thine eyes and do not contend with complaining words. (2 Tim. 2:14).

And if at present thou seem to be overcome, and to suffer a confusion which thou hast not deserved, do not repine at this and do not lessen thy crown by impatience.

Rather look up to Me in Heaven, who am able to deliver thee from all confusion and wrong, and to repay every one according to his works. (Matt. 16:27).

CHAPTER XXXVII
Resignation of Ourselves

CHRIST

SON, leave thyself and thou shalt find Me. Stand without choice or any self-seeking, and thou shalt always gain.

For greater grace shall always be added to thee, when thou hast perfectly given up thyself, without resuming thyself again.

DISCIPLE

2. Lord, how often shall I resign myself and in what things shall I leave myself?

CHRIST

3. Always and at all times, as in little, so also in great: I make no exception, but will have thee to be found in all things divested of thyself.

Otherwise how canst thou be Mine and I thine, unless thou be both within and without freed from all self-will?

The sooner thou effectest this the better will it be for thee;

and the more fully and sincerely thou dost it the more wilt thou please Me and the more shalt thou gain.

4. Some there are that resign themselves, but it is with some exception, for they do not trust wholly to God, and, therefore, are busy to provide for themselves.

Some also, at the first, offer all; but afterward, being assaulted by temptation, return again to what they left, and, therefore, they make no progress in virtue.

These shall not attain to the true liberty of a pure heart, nor to the grace of a delightful familiarity with Me, unless they first entirely resign themselves and offer themselves a daily sacrifice to Me; for without this, divine union neither is nor will be obtained.

5. I have often said to thee and I repeat it again, forsake thyself, resign thyself, and thou shalt enjoy a great inward peace. (Matt. 16:24).

Give all for all; seek nothing, call for nothing back; stand purely and with a full confidence in Me, and thou shalt possess Me.

Thou shalt be at liberty within thine own heart, and darkness shall not overwhelm thee.

Aim only at this, pray for this, desire this, that thou mayest be divested of all self-seeking; and, thus naked, follow thy naked Jesus; that thou mayest die to thyself and live eternally to Me.

Then shall vanish all vain imaginations, all evil disturbances and superfluous cares.

Then also immoderate fear shall leave thee and inordinate love shall die.

CHAPTER XXXVIII

Government of Ourselves

CHRIST

SON, thou must diligently make it thine aim, that in every place and in every action, or outward employment, thou be inwardly free and master of thyself, and that all things be under thee and not thou under them.

That thou mayest be lord and ruler of thine actions, not a slave or bondsman.

But rather a freeman and a true Hebrew, transferred to the lot and to the liberty of the children of God. (Rom. 8:21).

Who stand above the things present and contemplate those that are eternal.

Who look upon transitory things with the left eye, and with the right the things of Heaven.

Who suffer not themselves to be drawn away by temporal things to cleave to them, but rather draw these things to that end for which they were ordained by God and appointed by that sovereign artist, who has left nothing in all His works but what is regular and orderly.

2. If likewise, in all events, thou rule not thyself by the outward appearance, nor look on what thou seest or hearest with a carnal eye, but presently, on every occasion, dost enter, like Moses, into the tabernacle, to consult the Lord, thou shalt sometimes hear the divine answer and come out instructed in many things, present and to come.

For Moses always had recourse to the tabernacle, for the deciding of all doubts and questions, and fled to the help of prayer against the dangers and wickedness of men.

So must thou in like manner fly to the closet of thy heart, and there most earnestly implore the divine assistance. (Matt. 6:6).

For Josue, and the children of Israel, as we read, were therefore deceived by the Gabaonites because they did not first consult the Lord, but too easily giving credit to fair words were deluded with counterfeit piety. (Jos. 9:15).

CHAPTER XXXIX
Eagerness in Worldly Affairs

CHRIST

SON, always commit thy cause to Me; I will dispose well of it in due season. Wait for My disposal and thou shalt find it will be for thine advantage.

DISCIPLE

2. Lord, I willingly commit all things to Thee; for my care can profit little.

Would that I were not too much set upon future events, but offered myself with all readiness to Thy divine pleasure.

CHRIST

3. My son, oftentimes a man eagerly sets about a thing which he desires; but when he has obtained it he begins to be of another mind.

For men's inclinations are not wont to continue long upon the same thing, but rather pass from one thing to another.

It is therefore a thing of no little importance to forsake thyself even in the least things.

4. A man's true progress consists in denying himself, and the man who has renounced himself is much at liberty and very safe.

But the old enemy, who opposes all that is good, fails not to tempt; but day and night lays his dangerous plots to draw the unwary into his deceitful snares.

"Watch and pray," says the Lord, "that ye enter not into temptation." (Matt. 26:41).

CHAPTER XL

Man Cannot Glory in Anything

DISCIPLE

LORD, what is man that Thou art mindful of him; or the son of man that Thou visitest him? (Ps. 8:3).

What hath man deserved that Thou shouldst give him Thy grace?

Lord, what cause have I to complain if Thou forsake me? or what can I justly allege if Thou refuse to grant my petition?

This, indeed, I may truly think and say, Lord, I am nothing, I can do nothing, I have nothing of myself that is good; but I fail and am defective in all things, and ever tend to nothing.

And unless I am supported and interiorly instructed by Thee, I become quite tepid and dissolute.

2. But Thou, O Lord, art always the same and endurest forever; always good, just, and holy; doing all things well, justly, and holily; and disposing them in wisdom. (Wis. 12:13).

But I, who am more inclined to go back than to advance, continue not always in one state; for seven different seasons are changed over me. (Dan. 4:15).

Yet it quickly becomes better when it pleaseth Thee, and Thou stretchest out Thy helping hand; for Thou alone without man's aid can assist me, and so strengthen me that my countenance shall be no more changed in various ways, but my heart shall be converted and take its rest in Thee alone.

Wherefore, if I did but well know how to cast away from me all human comfort, either for the sake of devotion, or through the necessity of seeking Thee, because there is no man that can comfort me, then might I justly depend on Thy grace, and rejoice in the gift of new consolation.

Thanks be to Thee, from whom all proceeds, as often as it goes well with me.

But, for my part, I am but mere vanity, and nothing in Thy sight; an inconstant and weak man.

What have I then to glory in? or why do I desire to be esteemed?

Is it not for nothing? and this is most vain.

Truly vainglory is an evil plague, a very great vanity, because it draws us away from true glory, and robs us of heavenly grace.

For whilst a man takes complacency in himself, he displeaseth Thee; whilst he seeks after the praises of men, he is deprived of true virtues.

5. But true glory and holy joy is to glory in Thee and not in one's self; to rejoice in Thy name, and not to be delighted in one's own virtue, nor in any creature, save only for Thy sake.

Let Thy name be praised, not mine; let Thy work be extolled, not mine; let Thy holy name be blessed, but to me let nothing be attributed of the praises of men.

Thou art my glory, Thou art the joy of my heart.

In Thee will I glory and rejoice all the day; but for myself I will glory in nothing but in my infirmities. (2 Cor. 12:5).

6. Let the Jews seek the glory which one man receives from another; I will seek that which is from God alone. (John 5:44).

All human glory, all temporal honour, all worldly grandeur, compared to Thine eternal glory is but vanity and foolishness.

O my truth and my mercy, O my God, O blessed Trinity! to Thee alone be all praise, honour, power, and glory, for endless ages of ages. (Deut. 26:19).

CHAPTER XLI
Contempt for Temporal Honour

CHRIST

MY son, take it not to heart if thou see others honoured and advanced and thyself despised and debased.

Lift up thy heart to Me in Heaven and thou wilt not be concerned at thy being condemned by men upon earth.

DISCIPLE

2. Lord, we are in blindness, and are quickly seduced by vanity.

If I look well into myself, never was any injury done me by any creature, and therefore I cannot justly complain of Thee.

For, because I have often and grievously sinned against Thee, all creatures have reason to take up arms against me.

To me, therefore, confusion and contempt is justly due; but to Thee praise, honour, and glory. (Dan. 9:7; Bar. 1:15).

And unless I put myself in this disposition: to be willing to be despised and forsaken of all creatures, and to be esteemed nothing at all, I cannot arrive at inward peace and strength, nor be spiritually enlightened, nor fully united to Thee.

CHAPTER XLII
Peace is Not to be Placed in Men

CHRIST

SON, if thou place thy peace in any person, for the sake of thy contentment in his company, thou shalt be unsettled and entangled.

But if thou have recourse to the everlasting and subsisting truth, thou shalt not be grieved when a friend departs or dies.

In Me the love of thy friend must stand, and for Me he is to be loved whoever he be that appears to thee good, and is very dear to thee in this life.

Without Me no friendship is of any strength, nor will be durable; nor is that love true and pure of which I am not the bond.

Thou oughtest to be so far mortified to such affections of persons beloved, as to wish for, as much as appertains to thee, to be without any company of man.

A man draws nigher to God the farther he withdraws himself from all earthly comfort.

He ascends the higher into God, the lower he descends into himself, and the meaner he esteems himself.

2. But he that attributes anything of good to himself stops the grace of God from coming into him; for the grace of the Holy Ghost ever seeks an humble heart. (1 Ptr. 5:5).

If thou couldst perfectly annihilate thyself, and cast out from thyself all created love, then would abundance of grace flow into thee.

When thou lookest towards creatures the sight of the Creator is withdrawn from thee.

Learn, for the Creator's sake to, overcome thyself in all things, and then thou shalt be able to attain to the knowledge of God.

How little soever it be, if a thing be inordinately loved and regarded, it keeps thee back from the sovereign good and corrupts the soul.

CHAPTER XLIII
Against Vain Learning

CHRIST

SON, be not moved with the fine and subtle sayings of men, for the Kingdom of God is not in speech, but in power. (1 Cor. 4:20).

Attend to My words which inflame the heart and enlighten the mind, which excite to compunction and afford manifold consolations.

Never read anything that thou mayest appear more learned or more wise.

Study rather to mortify thy vices, for this will avail thee more than the being able to answer many hard questions.

2. When thou shalt have read, and shalt know many things, thou must always return to one beginning.

I am He that teach men knowledge, and I give a more clear understanding to little ones than can be taught by man. (Ps. 93:10).

He to whom I speak will quickly be wise, and will make great progress in spirit.

Woe to them that inquire of men after many curious things, and are little curious of the way to serve Me.

The time will come when Christ, the Master of masters, the Lord of angels, shall appear to hear the lessons of all men, that is, to examine the consciences of everyone.

And then He will search Jerusalem with candles (Soph. 1:12), and the hidden things of darkness shall be brought to light (1 Cor. 4:5), and the arguments of tongues shall be silent.

3. I am He that in an instant elevates an humble mind to comprehend more reasons of the eternal truth than could be

acquired by ten years' study in the schools.

I teach without noise of words, without confusion of opinions, without ambition of honour, without contention of arguments.

I teach to despise earthly things, to loathe things present, to seek and relish things eternal, to fly honours, to endure scandals, to repose all hope in Me, to desire nothing out of Me, and above all things, ardently to love Me.

4. For a certain person, by loving Me entirely, learned divine things and spoke wonders.

He profited more by forsaking all things than by studying subtleties.

But to some I speak things common, to others things more particular; to some I sweetly appear in signs and figures, to others in great light I reveal mysteries.

The voice of the books is the same, but it teacheth not all men alike; because I within am the teacher of truth, the searcher of hearts, the understander of thoughts, the promoter of actions; distributing to everyone as I judge fitting. (1 Cor. 12:1).

CHAPTER XLIV

Deadness to Exterior Things

CHRIST

SON, in many things it behooveth thee to be ignorant, and to esteem thyself as one dead upon earth; as one to whom the whole world is crucified.

Many things also must thou pass by with a deaf ear, and think rather of those things that appertain to thy peace.

It is more profitable to turn away thine eyes from such things as displease thee, and to leave to everyone his own way of thinking, than to give way to contentious discourses.

If thou stand well with God, and look at His judgment, thou wilt more easily bear to see thyself overcome.

DISCIPLE

2. O Lord, to what are we come? Behold a temporal loss is greatly bewailed; for a small gain men labour and toil, but the loss of the soul is little thought of, and hardly returns to mind.

That which is of little or no profit takes up our thoughts; and that which is above all things necessary, is negligently passed over; for the whole man sinks down into outward things, and unless he quickly recovers himself, he willingly continues immersed in them.

CHAPTER XLV

Men Are Prone to Offend

DISCIPLE

GRANT me help, O Lord, from trouble, for vain is the salvation of man. (Ps. 59:13).

How often have I not failed to find faith there where I thought I might depend upon it.

And how often have I found it where I did not expect it?

Vain, therefore, is all hope in men; but the safety of the just is in Thee, O Lord.

Blessed be Thou, O Lord my God, in all things that befall us.

We are weak and unsettled, we are quickly deceived and changed.

2. Who is the man that is able to keep him self so warily, and with so much circumspection in all things, as not to fall sometimes into some deceit or perplexity?

But he that trusts in Thee, O Lord, and seeks Thee with a

simple heart does not so easily fall (Wis. 1:1).

And if he fall into some tribulation, in what manner soever he may be entangled therein, he will quickly be rescued or comforted by Thee; for Thou wilt not forsake forever him that trusts in Thee. (Ps. 36:28).

A trusty friend is rarely to be found that continues faithful in all the distresses of his friend. (Ecclus. 6:10).

Thou, O Lord, Thou alone art most faithful in all things, and besides Thee, there is no other such.

3. Oh, how wise was that holy soul that said, My mind is strongly settled and grounded upon Christ. (Eph. 3:17).

If it were so with me the fear of man would not so easily give me trouble, nor flying words move me.

Who can foresee all things, or who is able to provide against all future evils?

If things foreseen do nevertheless often hurt us, how can things unlooked-for fail of wounding us grievously?

But why did I not provide better for myself, miserable wretch that I am! why also have I so easily given credit to others!

But we are men, and but frail men, though by many we are reputed and called angels.

To whom shall I give credit, O Lord? to whom but to Thee? Thou art the truth which neither canst deceive, nor be deceived. (John 14:6).

And on the other side, every man is a liar (Ps. 115:11), infirm, unstable, and subject to fail, especially in words; so that we ought not readily to believe even that which in appearance seems to sound well.

4. How wisely didst Thou forewarn us to beware of men (Matt. 10:17), and that a man's enemies are they of his own household (Matt. 36); and that we are not to believe, if anyone should say, "Behold here, or behold there." (Matt. 24:23).

I have been taught to my cost, and I wish it may serve to make me more cautious, and not to increase my folly.

"Be wary," saith one, "be wary, keep to thyself what I tell thee." And whilst I hold my peace, and believe the matter to be secret, he himself cannot keep the secret which he desires me to keep, but presently betrays both me and himself, and goes his way.

From such tales and such incautious people defend me, O Lord, that I may not fall into their hands, nor ever commit the like.

Give to my mouth truth and constancy in my words, and remove far from me a crafty tongue.

What I am not willing to suffer I ought by all means to shun.

5. Oh, how good a thing and how peaceable it is to be silent of others (Prov. 25:9), nor to believe all that is said, nor easily to report what one has heard:

To lay one's self open to few; always to seek Thee, the beholder of the heart;

Not to be carried about with every wind of words; but to wish that all things, both within and without us, may go according to the pleasure of Thy will.

How secure it is for the keeping of heavenly grace to fly the sight of men; and not to seek those things that seem to cause admiration abroad; but with all diligence to follow that which brings amendment of life and fervour.

To how many hath it been hurtful to have their virtue known and over-hastily praised.

How profitable indeed hath grace been kept with silence in this frail life! all which is a state of temptation and a warfare.

CHAPTER XLVI

Confidence in God

CHRIST

SON, stand firm and trust in Me; for what are words but words: they fly through the air, but hurt not a stone.

If thou art guilty, think that thou wilt willingly amend thyself.

If thy conscience accuse thee not, think that thou wilt willingly suffer this for God's sake.

It is a small matter that thou shouldst sometimes bear with words, if thou hast not as yet courage to endure hard stripes.

And why do such small things go to thy heart, but because thou art yet carnal, and regardest men more than thou oughtest!

For because thou art afraid of being despised, thou art not willing to be reprehended for thy faults, and seekest to shelter thyself in excuses.

2. But look better into thyself and thou shalt find that the world is still living in thee, and a vain desire of pleasing men.

For when thou art unwilling to be humbled and confounded for thy defects, it is plain indeed that thou art not truly humble, nor truly dead to the world, nor the world crucified to thee. (Gal. 6:14).

But give ear to My word, and thou shalt not value ten thousand words of men.

Behold, if all should be said against thee which the malice of men can invent, what hurt could it do thee if thou wouldst let it pass, and make no account of it? Could it even so much as pluck one hair from thee? (Luke 21:18).

3. But he who has not his heart within, nor God before his

eyes, is easily moved with a word of censure.

Whereas he that trusts in Me, and desires not to stand by his own judgment, will be free from the fear of men.

For I am the judge and discerner of all secrets, I know how the matter passeth; I know both him that offers the injury, and him that suffers it.

From Me this word went forth: by My permission it happened, that out of many hearts thoughts may be revealed. (Luke 2:35).

I shall judge the guilty and the innocent, but by a secret judgment I would beforehand try them both.

4. The testimony of men oftentimes deceives; My judgment is true, it shall stand and not be overthrown. (Ps. 18:10).

It is hidden for the most part, and to few laid open in everything; yet it never errs, nor can it err, even though to the eyes of the unwise it seem not right.

To Me, therefore, must thou run in every judgment and not depend upon thine own will.

For the just man will not be troubled whatever happens to him from God. (Prov. 12:21). And if anything be wrongfully pronounced against him he will not much care.

Neither will he vainly rejoice if by others he be reasonably excused.

For he considers that I am He that searcheth the heart and the reins (Ps. 7:10); who judgeth not according to the face, nor according to human appearance.

For oftentimes that is found culpable in My eyes which in the judgment of men is esteemed commendable.

Disciple

5. O Lord God, the just Judge, strong and patient, Who knowest the frailty and perverseness of men, be Thou my

strength and all my confidence, for my own conscience sufficeth me not.

Thou knowest that which I know not, and therefore in
every reprehension I ought to humble myself, and bear it
with meekness.

Pardon me, I beseech Thee, in Thy mercy, as often as I have
done thus, and give me again the grace to suffer still more.

For better to me is Thy plenteous mercy for the obtaining
of pardon, than the justice which I imagine in myself for the
defense of my hidden conscience.

Although my conscience accuse me not, yet I cannot hereby justify myself (1 Cor. 4:4); for setting Thy mercy aside, in
Thy sight no man living shall be justified. (Ps. 142:2).

CHAPTER XLVII

Things to be Endured

CHRIST

SON, be not dismayed with the labours which thou hast
undertaken for Me; neither let the tribulations which
befall thee quite cast thee down; but let My promise strength-
en thee, and comfort thee in every event. (Ps. 118:71).

I am sufficient to reward thee beyond all measure. (Gen.
15:1).

Thou shalt not labour here long, nor shalt thou be always
oppressed with sorrows.

Wait a little while and thou shalt see a speedy end of all
thine evils.

The hour will come when labour and trouble shall be no
more.

All is little and short which passeth away with time. (Wis.
3:9).

2. Do thy part well; mind what thou art about; labour

faithfully in My vineyard, I will be thy reward.

Write, read, sing, sigh, keep silence, pray, bear thy crosses manfully; eternal life is worthy of all these, and greater combats.

Peace shall come in one day, which is known to the Lord; and it shall not be a vicissitude of day and night, such as is at present; but everlasting light, infinite brightness, steadfast peace, and secure rest. (Apoc. 21:23).

Thou shalt not then say: Who shall deliver me from the body of this death? (Rom. 7:24). Nor shalt thou cry out: Woe is me, that my sojourning is prolonged. (Ps. 119:5). For death shall be no more, but never-failing health; no anxiety, but blessed delight; and a society sweet and lovely.

Oh, if thou hadst seen the everlasting crown of the saints in Heaven, and in how great glory they now triumph who appeared contemptible heretofore to this world, and in a manner even unworthy of life, doubtless thou wouldst immediately cast thyself down to the very earth, and wouldst rather seek to be under the feet of all, than to have command over so much as one.

Neither wouldst thou covet the pleasant days of this life, but wouldst rather be glad to suffer tribulation for God's sake, and esteem it thy greatest gain to be reputed as nothing amongst men.

3. Ah! if thou didst but relish these things, and suffer them to penetrate deeply into thy heart, how wouldst thou dare so much as once to complain!

Are not all painful labours to be endured for everlasting life?

It is no small matter to lose or gain the Kingdom of God.

Lift up therefore thy face to Heaven. Behold, I, and all My saints with Me, who in this world have had a great conflict, do now rejoice, are now comforted, are now secure, are now at rest, and they shall for all eternity abide with Me in the Kingdom of My Father. (Wis. 5:1).

CHAPTER XLVIII

Of the Day of Eternity

DISCIPLE

O MOST happy mansion of the city above! O most bright day of eternity, which knows no night, but is always enlightened by the sovereign truth! a day always joyful, always secure, and never changing its state for the contrary!

Oh, that this day would shine upon us, and all those temporal things would come to an end!

It shines indeed upon the saints, resplendent with everlasting brightness (Tob. 13:13), but to us pilgrims upon earth it is seen only as far off, and through a glass. (1 Cor. 13:12).

2. The citizens of Heaven know how joyful that day is; but the banished children of Eve lament that this our day is bitter and tedious.

The days of this life are short and evil (Gen. 48:9), full of sorrows and miseries: where man is defiled with many sins, is ensnared with many fears, disquieted with many cares, distracted with many curiosities, entangled with many vanities, encompassed with many errors, broken with many labours, troubled with temptations, weakened with delights, tormented with want.

3. Oh, when will there be an end of these evils? When shall I be set at liberty from the wretched slavery of sin? (Rom. 7:24).

When, O Lord, shall I think of Thee alone? When shall I to the full rejoice in Thee? (Ps. 69:5).

When shall I be without any impediment in true liberty, without any trouble of mind or body?

When shall I enjoy a solid peace never to be disturbed and always secure, a peace both within and without, a peace every way firm?

O good Jesus, when shall I stand to behold Thee? When shall I contemplate the glory of Thy Kingdom? When wilt Thou be all in all to me?

Oh, when shall I be with Thee in Thy Kingdom, which Thou hast prepared for Thy beloved for all eternity? (Matt. 25:34).

I am left a poor and banished man in an enemy's country, where there are wars every day, and very great misfortunes.

4. Comfort me in my banishment, assuage my sorrow; for all my desire is after Thee, and all that this world offers for my comfort is burdensome to me.

I long to enjoy Thee intimately, but cannot attain to it.

I desire to cleave to heavenly things, but the things of this life and my unmortified passions bear me down.

I am willing in mind to be above all things, but by the flesh am obliged against my will to be subject to them.

Thus, unhappy man that I am, I fight with myself, and am become burdensome to myself, whilst the spirit seeks to tend upwards, and the flesh downwards.

5. Oh, what do I suffer interiorly, whilst in my mind I consider heavenly things, and presently a crowd of carnal thoughts comes to interrupt my prayer? O God, be not Thou far from me (Ps. 70:12), and decline not in Thy wrath from Thy servant. (Ps. 26:9).

Dart forth lightning, and Thou shalt scatter them; shoot out Thine arrows (Ps. 143:6), and let all the phantoms of the enemy be put to flight.

Gather my senses together to Thee; make me forget all worldly things; give me the grace speedily to cast away and to despise all wicked imaginations.

Come to my aid, O eternal Truth, that no vanity may move me.

Come, heavenly sweetness, and let all impurity fly from before Thy face.

Pardon me also, and mercifully forgive me the times that I have thought of anything else in prayer besides Thee.

For I confess truly that I am accustomed to be very much distracted.

For oftentimes I am not there where I am bodily standing or sitting, but am rather where my thoughts carry me.

There I am where my thought is; and there oftentimes are my thoughts where that is which I love.

That thing most readily comes to my mind which naturally delights me, or which through custom is pleasing to me.

6. For this reason Thou who art the Truth hast plainly said, where thy treasure is, there also is thy heart. (Matt. 6:21).

If I love Heaven I willingly think on heavenly things.

If I love the world I rejoice in the prosperity of the world, and am troubled at its adversity.

If I love the flesh my imagination is often taken up with things of the flesh.

If I love the spirit I delight to think of spiritual things.

For whatsoever things I love, of the same I willingly speak and hear, and carry home with me the images of them.

But blessed is the man, who for Thee, O Lord, lets go all things created; who offers violence to his nature, and through fervour of spirit crucifies the lusts of the flesh: that so his conscience being cleared up, he may offer to Thee pure prayer, and may be worthy to be admitted among the choirs of angels, having excluded all things of the earth both from without and within.

CHAPTER XLIX
Desire of Eternal Life

CHRIST

SON, when thou perceivest a longing after eternal bliss to be infused into thee from above, and that thou desirest to go out of the dwelling of this body, that thou mayest contemplate My brightness, without any shadow of change (James 1:17), enlarge thy heart (Ps. 118:32), and with all thine affections embrace this holy inspiration.

Return very great thanks to the divine bounty, which deals so favourably with thee, which mercifully visits thee, ardently incites thee, and powerfully raises up; lest by thine own weight thou fall down to the things of the earth.

For it is not by thine own thought or endeavour that thou attainest to this; but only by the favour of heavenly grace and the divine visit: that so thou mayest advance in virtue and greater humility, and prepare thyself for future conflicts, and labour with the whole affection of thy heart to keep close to Me, and serve Me with a fervent will.

2. Son, the fire often burns, but the flame ascends not without smoke.

So also some people's desires are on fire after heavenly things, and yet they are not free from the temptation of carnal affection.

And therefore it is not altogether purely for God's honour that they do what they so earnestly request of Him.

Such also is oftentimes thy desire, which thou hast signified to be so strong.

For that is not pure and perfect which is infected with self-interest.

3. Ask not what is delightful and commodious for thee but

what is pleasing and honourable to Me; for if thou judgest rightly, thou oughtest to follow My appointment rather than thine own desire, and prefer it before all that thou desirest.

I know thy desire, and I have often heard thy sighs. (Ps. 37:10).

Thou wouldst be glad to be at present in the liberty of the glory of the children of God. (Rom. 5:2). Thou wouldst be pleased to be now at thine eternal home, and in thy heavenly country abounding with joy; but that hour is not yet come: for this is yet another time, a time of war, a time of labour and trial.

Thou wishest to be replenished with the sovereign good, but thou canst not at present attain to it.

I am that sovereign good; expect Me, saith the Lord (Soph. 3:8), till the Kingdom of God come. (Luke 22:18).

4. Thou must yet be tried upon earth and exercised in many things.

Consolation shall sometimes be given thee; but to be fully satisfied shall not be granted thee.

Take courage (Jos. 1:6), therefore, and be valiant as well in doing as in suffering things repugnant to thy nature.

Thou must put on the new man (Eph. 4:24), and be changed into another man.

Thou must oftentimes do that which is against thine inclination, and forego that to which thou art inclined.

That which is pleasing to others shall go forward; that which thou wouldst have shall not succeed.

That which others say shall be hearkened unto, what thou sayst shall not be regarded.

Others shall ask and shall receive, thou shalt ask and not obtain.

5. Others shall be great in the esteem of men; but of thee no notice shall be taken.

To others this or that shall be committed; but thou shalt be accounted fit for nothing.

At this nature will sometimes repine, and it will be no small matter if thou bear it with silence.

In these and many suchlike things the faithful servant of the Lord is used to be tried, how far he can renounce himself, and break himself in all things.

There is scarcely any one thing in which thou standest so much in need of mortifying thyself as in seeing and suffering the things which are repugnant to thy will, and especially when that is commanded which seems to thee incongruous and to little purpose.

And because being under authority thou darest not resist the higher power, therefore thou art apt to think it hard to walk at the beck of another, and wholly to give up thine own sentiment.

6. But consider, son, the fruit of these labours, how quickly they will end, and their exceeding great reward, and thou wilt not be troubled at them, but strongly comforted in thy suffering. (Heb. 6:18).

For, in regard to that little of thy will which thou now willingly forsakest, thou shalt forever have thy will in Heaven.

For there thou shalt find all that thou wiliest, all that thou canst desire.

There thou shalt enjoy all good without fear of ever losing it.

There thy will, being always one with Mine, shall desire nothing foreign or private.

There no one shall resist thee, no man shall complain of thee, none shall hinder thee, nothing shall stand in thy way: but all that thou desirest shall be there together present, and shall replenish thy whole affection, and satiate it to the full.

There I will give thee glory for the affronts which thou hast suffered; a garment of praise for thy sorrow (Is. 61:3), and for thy having been seated here in the lowest place, a royal throne for all eternity.

There will the fruit of obedience appear, there will the labour of penance rejoice, and humble subjection shall be gloriously crowned.

7. Bow down thyself then humbly at present under the hands of all, and heed not who it was that has said or commanded this.

But let it be thy great care that whether thy superior, inferior, or equal, desire anything of thee, or hint at anything, thou take all in good part and labour with a sincere will to perform it.

Let one man seek this, another that; let this man glory in this thing, another in that, and be praised a thousand times; but thou, for thy part, rejoice neither in this, nor in that, but in the contempt of thyself, and in My good pleasure and honour alone.

This is what thou oughtest to wish, that whether in life or death God may be always glorified in thee. (Phil. 1:20).

CHAPTER L
An Offering to God

Disciple

O LORD God, O holy Father, be Thou now and forever blessed, for as Thou wilt, so it has happened, and what Thou dost is always good.

Let Thy servant rejoice in Thee, not in himself, nor in any other; for Thou alone art true joy, Thou my hope and my crown, Thou my gladness and my honour, O Lord.

What hath Thy servant but what he hath received from Thee (1 Cor. 4:7), and this without any merit on his side? All things are Thine which Thou hast given, and which Thou hast made.

I am poor, and in labours from my youth (Ps. 87:16), and my soul is grieved even unto tears sometimes, and sometimes is disturbed within herself, by reason of the passions which encompass her.

2. I long for the joy of peace, I implore the peace of Thy children, who are fed by Thee in the light of Thy consolation.

If Thou give peace, if Thou infuse holy joy, the soul of Thy servant shall be full of melody and devout in Thy praise.

But if Thou withdraw Thyself, as Thou art very often accustomed to do, he will not be able to run in the way of Thy commandments; but rather must bow down his knees, and strike his breast, because it is not with him as it was yesterday and the day before, when Thy lamp shined over his head, and he was covered under the shadow of Thy wings from temptations rushing in upon him.

3. O just Father, holy, and always to be praised, the hour is come for Thy servant to be tried.

O Father, worthy of all love, it is fitting that Thy servant should at this hour suffer something for Thee.

O Father, always to be honoured, the hour is come which Thou didst foresee from all eternity, that Thy servant for a short time should be oppressed without, but always live within to Thee.

That he should be a little slighted and humbled, and should fall in the sight of men; that he should be severely afflicted with sufferings and diseases, that so he may rise again with Thee in the dawning of a new light, and be glorified in Heaven.

O holy Father, Thou hast so appointed and such is Thy will, and that has come to pass which Thou hast ordained.

4. For this is a favour to Thy friend, that he should suffer and be afflicted in this world for the love of Thee; how often-soever, and by whom soever Thou permittest it to fall upon him.

Without Thy counsel and providence, and without cause, nothing is done upon earth.

It is good for me, O Lord, that Thou hast humbled me that I may learn Thy justifications (Ps. 118:71), and that I may cast away from me all pride of heart and presumption.

It is advantageous for me that shame has covered my face, that I may rather seek my comfort from Thee than from men.

I have also learned hereby to fear Thine impenetrable judgments, Who afflictest the just together with the wicked; but not without equity and justice.

5. Thanks be to Thee that Thou hast not spared me in my sufferings, but hast bruised me with bitter stripes, inflicting pain, and sending distress both within and without.

And of all things under Heaven there is none can comfort me but Thou, O Lord, my God, the heavenly physician of souls, who scourgest and savest, leadest down to hell, and bringest up again. (Tob. 13:2).

Thy discipline is on me, and Thy rod shall instruct me.

6. Behold, dear Father, I am in Thy hands, I bow myself down under the rod of Thy correction.

Strike Thou my back and my neck, that I may bend my crookedness to Thy will.

Make me a pious and humble disciple of Thine, as Thou art wont well to do, that I may walk at Thy nod at all times.

To Thee I commit myself, and all that is mine, to be corrected by Thee; it is better to be chastised here than hereafter.

Thou knowest everything (Job 42:2), and there is nothing in man's conscience hidden from Thee.

Thou knowest things to come before they are done; and Thou hast no need to be taught or admonished by any one of those things that pass upon earth.

Thou knowest what is expedient for my progress, and how serviceable tribulation is to rub away the rust of sin.

Do with me according to Thy good pleasure; it is what I desire; and despise not my sinful life, to no one better or more clearly known than to Thyself alone.

7. Grant, O Lord, that I may know what I ought to know; that I may love what I ought to love; that I may praise that which is most pleasing to Thee; that I may esteem that which is valuable in Thy sight; that I may despise that which is despicable in Thine eyes.

Suffer me not to judge according to the sight of the outward eye, nor to give sentence according to the hearing of the ears of men that know not what they are about; but to determine both of visible and spiritual matters with true judgment, and above all things ever to seek Thy good will and pleasure.

8. The sentiments of men are often wrong in their judgments, and the lovers of this world are deceived in loving visible things alone.

What is man the better for being reputed greater by man?

One deceitful man deceives another; the vain deceives the vain, the blind deceives the blind, the weak the weak, whilst he extols him, and in truth, doth rather confound him, whilst he vainly praises him.

For as much as each one is in Thine eyes, so much is he, and no more, saith the humble St. Francis.

CHAPTER LI
Practice of Humble Works

CHRIST

SON, thou canst not always continue in the most fervent desire of virtue, nor stand in the highest degree of contemplation; but it must needs be that thou sometimes descend to lower things, by reason of original corruption, and that thou bear the burden of this corruptible life, even against thy will, and with irksomeness.

As long as thou carriest about with thee thy mortal body, thou shalt feel trouble and heaviness of heart.

Thou oughtest, therefore, as long as thou art in the flesh, oftentimes to bewail the burden of the flesh, for that thou canst not without intermission be employed in spiritual exercises and divine contemplation.

2. At these times it is expedient for thee to fly to humble and exterior works, and to recreate thyself in good actions, to look for My coming and My heavenly visitation with an assured hope; to bear with patience thy banishment, and the aridity of thy mind, till thou be visited again by Me, and delivered from all anguish.

For I will make thee forget thy pains and enjoy internal rest.

I will lay open before thee the pleasant fields of the Scriptures, that thy heart being enlarged thou mayest begin to run in the way of My Commandments. (Ps. 118:32).

And then thou shalt say that the sufferings of this time are not worthy to be compared with the glory to come which shall be revealed in us. (Rom. 8:18).

CHAPTER LII

Man Unworthy of Consolation

DISCIPLE

L ORD, I am not worthy of Thy consolation or any spiritual visitation; and therefore Thou dealest justly with me when Thou leavest me poor and desolate.

For if I could shed tears like a sea, yet should I not be worthy of Thy comfort.

Since I have deserved nothing but stripes and punishment, because I have grievously and often offended Thee, and in very many things sinned against Thee.

Therefore, according to all just reason I have not deserved the least of Thy comforts.

But Thou, Who art a good and merciful God, Who wilt not have Thy works perish, to show the richness of Thy goodness towards the vessels of mercy (Rom. 9:23), vouchsafest beyond all his deserts to comfort Thy servant above human measure.

For Thy consolations are not like the consolations of men.

2. What have I done, O Lord, that Thou shouldst impart Thy heavenly comfort to me?

I can remember nothing of good that I have ever done: but that I was always prone to vice and very slothful to amend.

It is the truth, and I cannot deny it. If I should say otherwise Thou wouldst stand against me, and there would be none to defend me.

What have I deserved for my sins but Hell and everlasting fire?

In truth I confess that I am worthy of all scorn and contempt, neither is it fitting that I should be named among Thy devout servants. And though I would fain not hear this, yet for truth's sake I will condemn myself for my sins, that so I may the easier obtain Thy mercy.

3. What shall I say who am guilty and full of all confusion?

I have not the face to say anything but this one word: I have sinned, O Lord, I have sinned; have mercy on me, and pardon me.

"Suffer me, therefore, that I may lament my sorrow a little before I go to a land that is covered with the mist of death." (Job 10:20).

What dost Thou chiefly require of a guilty and wretched sinner but that he should heartily repent and humble himself for his sins?

In true contrition and humility of heart is brought forth hope of forgiveness; a troubled conscience is reconciled; grace that was lost is recovered; a man is secured from the wrath to come, and God meets the penitent soul in the holy kiss of peace.

4. Humble contrition for sins is an acceptable sacrifice to Thee, O Lord (Ps. 1:19), of far sweeter odour in Thy sight than the burning of frankincense.

This is also that pleasing ointment which Thou wouldst have to be poured upon Thy sacred feet, for Thou never yet hast despised a contrite and humbled heart. (Ps. 1:19).

Here is a sure place of refuge from the face of the wrath of the enemy. Here whatever has been elsewhere contracted of uncleanness is amended and washed away.

CHAPTER LIII
The Grace of God

CHRIST

SON, My grace is precious; it suffers not itself to be mingled with external things, or earthly consolations.

Thou must, therefore, cast away every obstacle to grace if thou desire to have it infused into thee.

Choose a secret place to thyself; love to dwell with thyself alone; seek not to be talking with anyone; but rather pour forth devout prayers to God, that thou mayest keep thy mind in compunction, and thy conscience clean.

Esteem the whole world as nothing; prefer the attendance on God before all external things.

For thou canst not both attend to Me and at the same time delight thyself in transitory things.

Thou must withdraw from thine acquaintance, and those dear to thee, and keep thy mind disengaged from all temporal comfort.

So the blessed Apostle Peter beseeches the faithful of Christ to keep themselves as strangers and pilgrims in this world. (7 Ptr. 2:11).

2. Oh, what great confidence shall he have at the hour of his death who is not detained by an affection to anything in the world.

But an infirm soul is not yet capable of having a heart thus perfectly disengaged from all things, neither doth the sensual man understand the liberty of an internal man. (1 Cor. 2:14).

But if he will be spiritual indeed he must renounce as well those that are near him, as those that are afar off, and beware of none more than of himself.

If thou perfectly overcome thyself thou shalt with more ease subdue all things else.

The perfect victory is to triumph over one's self.

For he that keeps himself in subjection, so that his sensuality is ever subject to reason, and reason in all things obedient to Me, he is indeed a conqueror of himself, and lord of all the world.

3. If thou desire to mount thus high, thou must begin manfully, and set the axe to the root (Matt. 3:10), that thou mayest root out and destroy thy secret inordinate inclination to thyself, and to all selfish and earthly goods.

This vice, by which a man inordinately loves himself, is at the bottom of all that which is to be rooted out and overcome in thee; which evil being once conquered and brought under, a great peace and tranquillity will presently ensue.

But because there are few that labour to die perfectly to themselves and that fully aim beyond themselves, therefore do they remain entangled in themselves, nor can they be elevated in spirit above themselves.

But he that desires to walk freely with Me must mortify all his wicked and irregular affections, and must not cleave to anything created with any concupiscence or private love.

CHAPTER LIV

Nature and Grace

CHRIST

SON, observe diligently the motions of nature and grace; for they move very opposite ways, and very subtlely, and can hardly be distinguished but by a spiritual man, and one that is internally illuminated.

All men indeed aim at good, and pretend to something good in what they do and say: therefore, under the appearance of good, many are deceived.

2. Nature is crafty and draws away many; she ensnares and deceives them, and always in tends herself for her end.

But grace walks with simplicity, declines from all appearance of evil, offers no deceits, and does all things purely for God, in whom also she rests as in her last end.

3. Nature is not willing to be mortified, or to be restrained, or to be overcome, or to be subject; neither will she of her own accord be brought under.

But grace studies the mortification of her own self, resists sensuality, seeks to be subject, covets to be overcome, aims not at enjoying her own liberty, loves to be kept under discipline, and desires not to have the command over anyone; but under God ever to live, stand, and be; and for God's sake is ever ready humbly to bow down herself under all human creatures. (1 Ptr. 2:13).

4. Nature labours for her own interest, and considers what gain she may reap from another.

But grace considers not what may be advantageous and profitable to herself, but rather what may be profitable to many. (1 Cor. 10:33).					•

5. Nature willingly receives honour and respect: But grace faithfully attributes all honour and glory to God.

6. Nature is afraid of being put to shame and despised:

But grace is glad to suffer reproach for the name of Jesus. (Acts 5:41).

7. Nature loves idleness and bodily rest: But grace cannot be idle and willingly embraces labour. (1 Cor. 15:10).

8. Nature seeks to have things that are curious and fine, and does not care for things that are cheap and coarse:

But grace is pleased with that which is plain and humble, rejects not coarse things, nor refuses to be clad in old clothes.

9. Nature has regard to temporal things, rejoices at earthly gain, is troubled at losses, and is provoked at every slight injurious word:

But grace attends to things eternal, and cleaves not to those which pass with time; neither is she disturbed at the loss of things, nor exasperated with hard words, for she places her treasure and her joy in Heaven, where nothing is lost.

10. Nature is covetous, and is more willing to take than to give, and loves to have things to herself:

But grace is bountiful and openhearted, avoids selfishness, is contented with little, and judges it a more blessed thing to give rather than to receive. (Acts 20:35).

11. Nature inclines to creatures, to her own flesh, to vanities, and to gadding abroad:

But grace draws to God and to virtue, renounces creatures, flies the world, hates the desires of the flesh, restrains wandering about, and is ashamed to appear in public.

12. Nature willingly receives exterior comfort, in which she may be sensibly delighted:

But grace seeks to be comforted in God alone, and beyond all things visible to be delighted in the Sovereign Good.

13. Nature doth all for her own lucre and interest; she can do nothing gratis, but hopes to gain something equal, or better, or praise, or favour for her good deeds; and covets to have her actions and gifts much valued:

But grace seeks nothing temporal, nor requires any other recompense but God alone for her reward, nor desires anything more of the necessaries of this life than may be serviceable in attaining a happy eternity.

14. Nature rejoices in a multitude of friends and kindred; she glories in the nobility of her stock and descent; she fawns on them that are in power, flatters the rich, and applauds such as are like herself:

But grace loves even her enemies, and is not puffed up with having a great many friends, nor esteems family or birth, unless when joined with greater virtue.

She rather favours the poor than the rich; she has more compassion for the innocent than the powerful; she rejoices with him that loves the truth, and not with the deceitful.

She ever exhorts the good to be zealous for better gifts, and to become like unto the Son of God by the exercise of virtues.

15. Nature easily complains of want and of trouble:

But grace bears poverty with constancy.

16. Nature turns all things to herself and for herself she labours and disputes:

But grace refers all things to God, from whom all originally proceed; she attributes no good to herself, nor does she arrogantly presume of herself; she does not contend, nor prefer her own opinion to others, but in every sense and understanding she submits herself to the eternal wisdom, and to the divine examination.

17. Nature covets to know secrets, and to hear news: is willing to appear abroad, and to have experience of many things by the senses; desires to be taken notice of, and to do such things as may procure praise and admiration.

But grace cares not for the hearing of new and curious things, because all this springs from the old corruption, since nothing is new or lasting upon earth.

She teaches, therefore, to restrain the senses, to avoid vain complacency and ostentation, humbly to hide those things which are worthy of praise and admiration, and from everything and in every knowledge to seek the fruit of spiritual profit, and the praise and honour of God.

She desires not to have herself or what belongs to her extolled; but wishes that God may be blessed in His gifts, who bestows all through mere love.

18. This grace is a supernatural light and a certain special gift of God, and the proper mark of the elect, and pledge of eternal salvation, which elevates a man from the things of the earth to the love of heavenly things, and from carnal makes him spiritual.

Wherefore, the more nature is kept down and subdued, the greater abundance of grace is infused; and the inward man, by new visitations, is daily more reformed according to the image of God. (Col. 3:10).

CHAPTER LV
The Corruption of Nature

DISCIPLE

O LORD, my God, Who hast created me to Thine own image and likeness, grant me this grace, which Thou hast declared to be so great, and so necessary to salvation, that I may overcome my corrupt nature, which draws me to sin and perdition.

For I perceive in my flesh the law of sin contradicting the law of my mind (Rom. 7:23), and leading me captive to obey sensuality in many things; neither can I resist the passions thereof unless assisted by Thy most holy grace, infused copiously into my heart.

2. I stand in need of Thy grace, and of a great grace, to overcome nature, which is always prone to evil from her youth.

For the first man, Adam, being corrupted by sin, the punishment of his sin has descended upon all mankind: so that nature itself, which by Thee was created good and right, is now put for the vice and infirmity of corrupt nature; because the motion thereof, left to itself, draws to evil, and to things below.

For the little strength which remains is but like a spark hidden in the ashes.

This is our natural reason, which is surrounded with a great mist, having yet the judgment of good and evil, and of the distance of truth and falsehood, though it be unable to fulfill all that it approves; neither does it now enjoy the full light of truth, nor the former purity of its affections.

3. Hence it is, O my God, that according to the inward man, I am delighted with Thy law (Rom. 7:22), knowing Thy command to be good, just, and holy, and reproving all evil and sin, as what ought to be shunned.

And yet in the flesh I serve the law of sin, whilst I rather obey sensuality than reason.

Hence it is, that to will is present with me, but to accomplish that which is good, I find not. (Rom. 7:18).

Hence I often make many good purposes: but because I want grace to help my weakness, through a slight resistance I recoil and fall off.

Hence it comes to pass, that I know the way to perfection, and see clearly enough what it is I ought to do.

But being pressed down with the weight of my own corruption I rise not to those things which are more perfect.

4. Oh, how exceedingly necessary is Thy grace for me, O Lord, to begin that which is good, to go forward with it, and to accomplish it!

For without it I can do nothing; but I can do all things in Thee, when Thy grace strengthens me. (Phil. 4:13).

O truly heavenly grace, without which we have no merits of our own, neither are any of the gifts of nature to be valued.

No arts, no riches, no beauty or strength, no wit or eloquence, are of any worth with Thee, O Lord, without grace.

For the gifts of nature are common to the good and bad;

but grace or divine love is the proper gift of the elect, and they that are adorned with it are esteemed worthy of eternal life.

This grace is so excellent that neither the gift of prophecy, nor the working of miracles, nor any speculation, how sublime soever, is of any value without it.

Nor even faith, nor hope, nor any other virtues, are acceptable to Thee without charity and grace.

5. O most blessed grace, which makest the poor in spirit rich in virtues, and renderest him who is rich in many good things humble of heart.

Come, descend upon me, replenish me betimes with Thy consolation, lest my soul faint through weariness and dryness of mind.

I beseech Thee, O Lord, that I may find grace in Thy sight (Gen. 18:3), for Thy grace is enough for me (2 Cor. 12:9), though I obtain none of those other things which nature desires.

If I be tempted and afflicted with many tribulations I will fear no evil whilst Thy grace is with me.

She is my strength; she gives counsel and help.

She is mightier than all my enemies, and wiser than all the wise.

6. She is the mistress of truth, the teacher of discipline, the light of the heart, the comforter of affliction, the banisher of sorrow, the expeller of fears, the nurse of devotion, the producer of tears.

What am I without her but a piece of dry wood, and an unprofitable stock, fit for nothing but to be cast away?

Let Thy grace, therefore, O Lord, always both go before me and follow me and make me ever intent upon good works, through Jesus Christ Thy Son. Amen.

CHAPTER LVI
On Self Denial

CHRIST

SON, as much as thou canst go out of thyself, so much wilt thou be able to enter into Me.

As desiring nothing abroad brings peace at home, so relinquishing thyself joins thee interiorly to God.

I will have thee learn the perfect renunciation of thyself, according to My will, without contradiction or complaint.

Follow Me (John 21:19): I am the way, the truth, and the life. (John 14:6). Without the way there is no going; without the truth there is no knowing; without the life there is no living.

I am the way which thou must follow; the truth which thou must believe; the life for which thou must hope.

I am the way inviolable, the truth infallible, and the life interminable.

I am the straightest way, the sovereign truth, the true life, the blessed life, and uncreated life.

If thou continue in My way thou shalt know the truth, and the truth shall deliver thee (John 8:32), and thou shalt attain to life everlasting. (Matt. 19:29).

2. If thou wilt enter into life, keep the Commandments. (Matt. 19:17).

If thou wilt know the truth, believe Me. (John 14:17).

If thou wilt be perfect, sell all things. (Matt. 19:21).

If thou wilt be My disciple, deny thyself. (Matt. 16:24).

If thou wilt possess a blessed life, despise this present life. (Matt. 16:25).

If thou wilt be exalted in Heaven, humble thyself in this world. (Matt. 18:4).

If thou wilt reign with Me, bear the cross with Me.

For none but the servants of the cross find the way of bliss and true light.

DISCIPLE

3. Lord Jesus, forasmuch as Thy way is narrow, and despised by the world, grant that I may follow Thee, and be despised by the world.

For the servant is not greater than his lord, neither is the disciple above his master. (Matt. 10:24).

Let Thy servant meditate on Thy life, for there is my salvation and true holiness.

Whatever I read or hear besides does not recreate nor fully delight me.

CHRIST

4. Son, now thou knowest these things and hast read them all, happy shalt thou be if thou fulfill them.

"He that hath my commandments, and keepeth them, he it is that loveth me; and I will love him, and will manifest myself unto him" (John 14:21), and "I will make him sit with me in the kingdom of my Father." (Matt. 19:28).

DISCIPLE

5. Lord Jesus, as Thou hast said and hast promised, so may it be indeed, and may it be my lot to merit it.

I have received the cross, I have received it from Thy hand; I will bear it, yea, I will bear it until death, as Thou hast laid it upon me.

Indeed the life of a good religious man is a cross, but it is a cross that conducts him to Paradise.

We have now begun, it is not lawful to go back, nor may we leave off. (Luke 9:62).

6. Take courage, my brethren, let us go forward together, Jesus will be with us. (Heb. 12:1).

For the sake of Jesus we took up His cross; for the sake of Jesus let us persevere on the cross.

He will be our helper, who is our captain and our leader.

Behold our King marches before us, who will fight for us.

Let us follow Him manfully; let no one shrink through fear; let us be ready to die valiantly in battle, and not stain our glory by flying from the standard of the cross. (1 Mach. 9:10).

CHAPTER LVII

Evils of Dejection

CHRIST

SON, patience and humility in adversity are more pleasing to Me than much consolation and devotion in prosperity.

Why art thou disturbed at a little thing said against thee?

If it had been more thou oughtest not to have been moved.

But now let it pass, it is not the first, or anything new, nor will it be the last, if thou live long.

Thou art valiant enough so long as no adversity or opposition comes in thy way.

Thou canst also give good advice, and encourage others with thy words; but when any unexpected trouble comes to knock at thy door then thy counsel and thy courage fail thee.

Consider thy great frailty which thou dost often experience in small difficulties; yet it is intended for thy good as often as these or such like things befall thee.

2. Put it from thy heart the best thou canst; and if it has

touched thee, yet let it not cast thee down, nor keep thee a long time entangled.

At least bear it patiently, if thou canst not receive it with joy.

And though thou be not willing to bear it, and perceivest an indignation arising within thyself, yet repress thyself, and suffer no inordinate word to come out of thy mouth, which may scandalize the weak.

The commotion which is stirred up in thee will quickly be allayed, and thine inward pain will be sweetened by the return of grace.

I am still living, saith the Lord, ready to help thee, and comfort thee more than before, if thou put thy trust in Me, and devoutly call upon Me.

3. Keep thy mind calm and even (Mark 10:49), and prepare thyself for bearing still more.

All is not lost if thou feel thyself often afflicted, or grievously tempted.

Thou art man and not a god; thou art flesh, and not an angel.

How canst thou think to continue ever in the same state of virtue, when this was not found in the angels of heaven, nor in the first man in paradise?

I am He who raises up and saves those who mourn; and those who know their own infirmity I advance to My divinity.

Disciple

4. O Lord, blessed be this Thy word, it is more sweet to my mouth than honey and the honeycomb. (Ps. 18:11).

What should I do in such great tribulation and anguish if Thou didst not encourage me with Thy holy words?

What matter is it how much or what I suffer, so I come at length to the haven of salvation?

Grant me a good end, grant me a happy passage out of this world.

Remember me, O my God, and direct me by the straight road to Thy Kingdom.

CHAPTER LVIII
Searching into High Matters

CHRIST

SON, see thou dispute not of high matters, nor of the hidden judgments of God: why this man is left thus, and this other is raised to so great a grace, or why this person is so much afflicted and that other so highly exalted.

These things are above the reach of man, neither can any reason or discourse penetrate into the judgments of God.

When, therefore, the enemy suggests to thee such things as these, or thou hearest curious men inquiring into them, answer with the Prophet: "Thou art just, O Lord: and thy judgment is right." (Ps. 118:137).

And again: "The judgments of the Lord are true, justified in themselves." (Ps. 18:10).

My judgments are to be feared, not to be searched into; for they are incomprehensible to human understanding. (Rom. 11:23).

2. In like manner do not inquire nor dispute concerning the merits of the saints, which of them is more holy than the other, or which greater in the Kingdom of Heaven. (Matt. 18:1).

These things oftentimes breed strife and unprofitable contentions, and nourish pride and vainglory; whence arise envy and dissensions, this man proudly seeking to prefer this saint, and another man preferring another.

To desire to know and to search into such things as these

is of no profit, but rather displeaseth the saints; for I am not the God of dissension but of peace (1 Cor. 14:33), which peace consists more in true humility than in exalting one's self.

3. Some are carried by a zeal of love towards these or those, with greater affection, but this affection is rather human than divine.

I am He who made all the saints; I gave them grace; I have brought them to glory.

I know the merits of each of them; I have prevented them with blessings of My sweetness. (Ps. 20:4).

I foreknew My beloved ones before the creation; I chose them out of the world; they were not beforehand to choose Me. (John 15:16).

I called them by My grace, and drew them by My mercy;

I led them safe through many temptations.

I imparted to them extraordinary comforts, I gave them perseverance, I have crowned their patience.

4. I know the first and the last: I embrace them all with an inestimable love.

I am to be praised in all My saints (Ps. 67:36), I am to be blessed above all things (Dan. 3:52), and to be honored in every one of them whom I have thus gloriously magnified and eternally chosen, without any foregoing merits of their own.

He, therefore, that despises one of the least of My saints, honors not the greatest, for both little and great I have made. (Wis. 6:7).

And he that derogates from any one of the saints derogates also from Me, and from all the rest of them in the Kingdom of Heaven.

They are all one through the bond of love; they have the same sentiments, the same will, and all mutually love one another. (John 17:21).

5. And yet, which is much higher, they all love Me more than themselves and their own merits.

For being elevated above themselves, and drawn out of the love of themselves, they are wholly absorbed in the love of Me, in whom also they rest by an eternal enjoyment.

Nor is there anything which can divert them from Me, or depress them; for being full of the eternal truth, they burn with the fire of charity that cannot be extinguished.

Therefore, let carnal and sensual men, who know not how to love anything but their private satisfactions, forbear to dispute of the state of the saints. They add and take away according to their own inclinations, not according to what is pleasing to the everlasting truth.

6. In many there is ignorance, especially in such as, being but little enlightened, seldom know how to love anyone with a perfect spiritual love.

They are as yet much inclined to these or those by a natural affection, and human friendship; and as they are affected with regard to things below they conceive the like imaginations of the things of Heaven.

But there is an incomparable distance between what the imperfect imagine and what the illuminated contemplate by revelation from above.

7. Take heed, therefore, My son, that thou treat not curiously of these things which exceed thy knowledge, but rather make it thy business and thine aim that thou be found even the least amongst those who inherit the Kingdom of God.

And if anyone should know who were more holy or greater in the Kingdom of Heaven, what would this knowledge profit him unless he would take occasion from knowing this, to humble himself in My sight, and to praise My name with greater fervour?

It is much more acceptable to God for a man to think of

the greatness of his own sins, and how little he is advanced
in virtue, and at how great a distance he is from the perfection of the saints, than to dispute which of them is greater or
less.

It is better to invoke the saints with devout prayers and
tears, and to implore their glorious suffrages with an humble
mind, than by a vain inquiry to search into their secrets.

8. They are well and perfectly contented, if men would but
be contented and refrain from their vain discourses.

They glory not in their own merits, for they ascribe nothing
of goodness to themselves, but all to Me, because I bestowed
all upon them out of My infinite charity.

They are filled with so great a love of the Deity, and such
overflowing joy, that there is nothing wanting to their glory,
nor can any happiness be wanting to them.

All the saints, the higher they are in glory the more humble
are they in themselves, and nearer to Me, and better beloved
by Me.

Therefore, thou hast it written, that they cast down their
crowns before God, and fell upon their faces before the
Lamb, and adored Him that liveth forever and ever. (Apoc.
4:10; 5:14).

9. Many examine who is greatest in the Kingdom of God,
who know not whether they shall be worthy to be numbered
among the least.

It is a great matter to be even the least in Heaven, where all
are great, because all shall be called, and shall be the children
of God. (Matt. 5:9).

The least shall be as a thousand, and the sinner of a hundred years shall die. (Is. 60:22; 65:20).

For when the disciples asked who was the greatest in the
Kingdom of Heaven they received this answer:

"Unless you be converted, and become as little children,

you shall not enter into the kingdom of heaven. Whosoever therefore shall humble himself as this little child, he is the greater in the kingdom of heaven." (Matt. 18:3).

10. Woe to those who disdain to humble themselves willingly with little children; for the low gates of the heavenly Kingdom will not suffer them to enter therein.

Woe also to the rich, who have their consolation here (Luke 6:24), for when the poor shall go into the Kingdom of God they shall stand lamenting without.

Rejoice you that are humble, and be glad you that are poor, for yours is the Kingdom of God (Matt. 5:3): yet so, if you walk in truth.

CHAPTER LIX
All Our Hope in God.

DISCIPLE

LORD, what is my confidence which I have in this life? or what is my greatest comfort amongst all things that appear under Heaven?

Is it not Thou, my Lord God, Whose mercies are without number?

Where was I ever well without Thee? or when could things go ill with me when Thou wast present?

I had rather be poor for Thee than rich without Thee.

I choose rather to sojourn upon earth with Thee than to possess Heaven without Thee. Where Thou art there is Heaven; and there is death and Hell where Thou art not.

After Thee I have a longing desire, and therefore must needs sigh after Thee, and cry and pray.

In fine, I cannot fully trust to anyone to bring me seasonable help in my necessities, save only to Thee, my God.

Thou art my hope, Thou art my confidence, Thou art my

comforter, and most faithful above all.

2. All seek their own interest; Thou aimest only at my salvation and profit, and turnest all things to my good. (Rom. 8:28).

And although Thou expose me to various temptations and adversities, yet all this Thou ordainest for my good, Who art wont to prove Thy beloved servants a thousand ways.

Under which proofs Thou oughtest not less to be loved and praised, than if Thou wert to fill me with heavenly comforts.

3. In Thee, therefore, O Lord God, I put all my hope and refuge; to Thee I make known all my tribulations and anguish (Ps. 31:7); for I find all to be infirm and unstable whatever I behold out of Thee.

For neither will a multitude of friends be of any service to me; nor can strong auxiliaries bring me any succour, nor wise counsellors give me a profitable answer, nor the books of the learned comfort me, nor any wealth deliver me, nor any secret and pleasant place secure me, if Thou Thyself do not assist, help, strengthen, comfort, instruct, and defend me.

4. For all things which seem to be for our peace and for our happiness, when Thou art absent, are nothing; and in truth contribute nothing to our felicity.

Thou, therefore, art the foundation of all good, the height of life, and the depth of wisdom; and to trust in Thee above all things is the greatest comfort of Thy servant.

To Thee I lift up mine eyes; in Thee, O my God, the Father of mercies, I put my trust. (Ps. 140:8).

Bless and sanctify my soul with Thy heavenly blessings, that it may be made Thy holy habitation, and the seat of Thine eternal glory; and let nothing be found in the temple of Thy dignity that may offend the eyes of Thy majesty.

According to the greatness of Thy goodness, and the multitude of Thy tender mercies, look down upon me (Ps. 68:17), and give ear to the prayer of Thy poor servant, who is in banishment afar off from Thee in the region of the shadow of death.

Protect and defend the soul of Thy poor servant, amidst the many dangers of this corruptible life, and direct him in the company of Thy grace, through the way of peace, to the country of everlasting light. Amen.

BOOK IV

Of the Blessed Sacrament

"COME to me all you that labour and are burdened and I will refresh you." (Matt. 11:28).

"The bread that I will give is my flesh, for the life of the world." (John 6:52).

"Take ye and eat; this is my body, which shall be delivered for you; this do for the commemoration of me." (1 Cor. 11:24).

"He that eateth my flesh, and drinketh my blood, abideth in me, and I in him." (John 6:57).

"The words that I have spoken to you are spirit and life." (John 6:64).

CHAPTER I

How Christ is to be Received

Disciple

THESE are Thy words, O Christ, the eternal truth, though not all delivered at one time, nor written in one place.

Since, therefore, they are Thy words, and true, they are all to be received by me with thanks and with faith.

They are Thine, and Thou hast spoken them; and they are also mine because Thou hast delivered them for my salvation.

I willingly received them from Thy mouth, that they may be more inseparably ingrafted in my heart.

These words of such great tenderness, full of sweetness and love, encourage me; but my sins terrify me, and my unclean conscience keeps me back from approaching such great mysteries.

The sweetness of Thy words invites me, but the multitude of my offences weighs me down.

2. Thou commandest me to approach to Thee with confidence if I would have part with Thee; and to receive the food of immortality if I desire to obtain life and glory everlasting.

"Come," sayest Thou to me, "all you that labour and are burdened, and I will refresh you." (Matt 11:28).

O sweet and amiable word in the ear of a sinner, that Thou, O Lord my God, shouldst invite the poor and needy to the Communion of Thy most sacred Body!

But who am I, O Lord, that I should presume to come to Thee?

Behold, the Heaven of heavens cannot contain Thee (3 Kgs. 8:27); and Thou sayest, "Come you all to Me."

3. What means this most loving condescension, and so friendly invitation?

How shall I dare to approach, who am conscious to myself of no good on which I can presume?

How shall I introduce Thee into my house, who have oftentimes provoked Thine indignation?

The angels and the archangels stand with a reverential awe; the saints and the just are afraid; and Thou sayest, "Come you all to Me."

Unless Thou, O Lord, didst say it, who could believe it to be true?

And unless Thou didst command it, who would dare attempt to approach?

4. Behold Noe, a just man (Gen. 6:9), laboured a hundred years in building the ark, that he with a few might be preserved; and how shall I be able in the space of one hour to prepare myself to receive with reverence the Maker of the world?

Moses Thy servant, Thy great and special friend, made an ark of incorruptible wood, which he also covered with the most pure gold, that he might deposit therein the tables of the law; and shall I, a rotten creature, presume so easily to receive Thee, the Maker of the law, and the Giver of life?

Solomon, the wisest of the kings of Israel, employed seven years in building a magnificent temple for the praise of Thy name:

And for eight days together celebrated the feast of the dedication thereof; he offered a thousand victims as peace offerings, and brought the Ark of the Covenant in a solemn manner into the place prepared for it, with sound of trumpet and jubilee. (3 Kgs. 8:6).

And I, a wretch, and the vilest of men, how shall I bring Thee into my house, who can hardly spend one half hour devoutly? And would I had even once spent one half hour itself as I ought!

5. O my God, how much did they endeavour to do to please Thee!

Alas! how little is what I do! How short a time do I spend when I prepare myself to communicate, being seldom wholly recollected, very seldom free from all distraction!

And yet, surely in the life-giving presence of Thy Deity, no unbecoming thought should occur, nor anything created take up my mind; for it is not an angel, but the Lord of angels that I am to entertain.

And yet there is a very great difference between the Ark of the Covenant with its relics, and Thy most pure Body, with its unspeakable virtues; between those sacrifices of the law, which were figures of things to come, and the true sacrifice of Thy Body, which is the accomplishing of all those ancient sacrifices.

Why then am I not more inflamed, considering Thy venerable presence?

Why do I not prepare myself with greater care to receive Thy sacred gifts, seeing that these ancient holy patriarchs and prophets, yea kings also and princes, with the whole people, have shown so great an affection of devotion towards Thy divine worship?

8. The most devout King David danced before the ark of God with all his might (2 Kgs. 6:14), commemorating the benefits bestowed in times past on the fathers. He made musical instruments of sundry kinds; he published psalms, and appointed them to be sung with joy; he himself likewise often sang them, playing upon his harp, inspired with the grace of the Holy Ghost. He taught the people of Israel to praise God with their whole heart, and to join their voices in blessing and magnifying Him every day.

If such great devotion was then used, and such remembrance of the praise of God before the Ark of the Covenant, how great ought to be the reverence and devotion which I and all Christian people should have in the presence of this Sacrament, and in receiving the most excellent Body of Christ!

9. Many run to sundry places to visit the relics of the saints, and are astonished to hear their wonderful works; they behold the noble church buildings and kiss their sacred bones, wrapt up in silk and gold.

And behold I have Thee here present on the altar, my God, the Saint of saints, the Creator of men, and the Lord of angels.

Oftentimes in seeing these things men are moved with curiosity, and the novelty of the sight, and but little fruit of amendment is reaped thereby; especially when persons lightly run hither and thither, without true contrition for their sins.

But here, in the Sacrament of the Altar, Thou art wholly present, my God, the man Christ Jesus; where also the fruit of eternal salvation is plentifully reaped, as often as Thou art worthily and devoutly received.

And to this we are not drawn by any levity, curiosity, or sensuality; but by a firm faith, a devout hope, and a sincere charity.

10. O God, the invisible Maker of the world, how wonderfully dost Thou deal with us! How sweetly and graciously dost Thou order all things in favour of Thine elect, to whom Thou offerest Thyself to be received in this Sacrament!

For this exceeds all understanding of man; this in a particular manner engages the hearts of the devout, and enkindles their love.

For Thy true faithful, who dispose their whole life to amendment, by this most worthy Sacrament, frequently receive a great grace of devotion and love of virtue.

11. Oh, the wonderful and hidden grace of this Sacrament, which only the faithful of Christ know; but unbelievers and such as are slaves to sin cannot experience.

In this Sacrament is conferred spiritual grace; lost virtue is repaired in the soul; and beauty disfigured by sin returns again.

And so great sometimes is this grace that from the abundance of the devotion that is bestowed, not only the mind, but the frail body also feels a great increase of strength.

12. Yet it is much to be lamented and pitied that we should be so lukewarm and negligent as not to be drawn with greater affection to the receiving of Christ, in whom consists all the hope and merit of those that shall be saved.

For He is our sanctification and our redemption; He is our comfort in our pilgrimage, and the eternal beatitude of the saints.

It is therefore much to be lamented that many esteem so lightly this saving mystery which rejoices Heaven and preserves the whole world.

Oh, the blindness and hardness of the heart of man that

doth not more highly prize so unspeakable a gift; and from daily use falls into a disregard of it.

13. For if this most holy Sacrament were only celebrated in one place, and consecrated by only one priest in the world, how great a desire would men have to go to that place, and to such a priest of God; that they might see the divine mysteries celebrated?

But now there are made many priests, and Christ is offered up in many places, that the grace and love of God to man may appear the greater, the more this sacred Communion is spread throughout the world.

Thanks be to Thee, O good Jesus, our eternal Shepherd, Who hast vouchsafed to feed us poor exiles with Thy precious Body and Blood, and to invite us to the receiving these mysteries with the very words of Thine Own mouth, saying, "Come to me all you that labour and are burdened, and I will refresh you." (Matt. 11:28).

CHAPTER II

The Great Goodness of God

Disciple

O LORD, trusting in Thy goodness, and in Thy great mercy, I come sick to my Saviour, hungry and thirsty to the fountain of life, needy to the King of Heaven, a servant to his lord, a creature to his Creator, and one in desolation to his tender comforter.

But whence is this to me, that Thou shouldst come to me? Who am I that Thou shouldst give Thyself to me?

How dare such a sinner appear before Thee? And Thou, how dost Thou vouchsafe to come to a sinner?

Thou knowest Thy servant, and Thou knowest that he has nothing of good in him that can entitle him to this favour.

I confess therefore my unworthiness, I acknowledge Thy bounty, I praise Thy goodness, and I give Thee thanks for Thine excessive charity.

For out of Thine own mercy Thou dost this, not for my merits, that Thy goodness may be better known to me; that greater charity may be imparted, and humility more perfectly recommended.

Since, therefore, this pleaseth Thee, and Thou hast commanded it should be so, Thy merciful condescension pleaseth me also but, oh! that my iniquity may be no obstacle.

2. O most sweet and most bountiful Jesus, what great reverence and thanks, with perpetual praise, are due to Thee for the receiving of Thy sacred Body, whose dignity no man can sufficiently express!

But what shall I think on in this communion, when I am approaching to my Lord, whom I can never reverence so much as I ought, and yet long to receive with devotion.

What can I think on better or more wholesome to my soul than to humble myself entirely in Thy presence, and extol Thine infinite goodness above me?

I praise Thee, O my God, and I extol Thee forever; I despise myself and subject myself to Thee, casting myself down to the depth of my unworthiness.

3. Behold Thou art the Saint of saints, and I am the greatest of sinners.

Behold Thou bowest Thyself down to me, who am not worthy to look up to Thee.

Behold Thou comest to me; Thou art willing to be with me; Thou invitest me to Thy banquet.

Thou wilt give me Thy heavenly food, and the bread of angels to eat (Ps. 77:25); no other, verily, than Thyself, the Living Bread, Who didst come down from Heaven, and Who givest life to the world. (John 6:33,41).

4. Behold whence love proceeds; what a bounty shines forth! What great thanks and praises are due to Thee for these things!

Oh, how wholesome and profitable was Thy design in this institution! how sweet and delightful this banquet, in which Thou givest Thyself to be our food!

Oh, how admirable is Thy work, O Lord! how powerful Thy virtue! how ineffable Thy truth!

For Thou hast spoken, and all things were made; and that has been done which Thou didst command.

5. A wonderful thing it is, and worthy of faith, and exceeding all human understanding, that Thou, O Lord my God, true God, and true man, art contained whole and entire under a small form of bread and wine, and without being consumed, art eaten by the receiver.

Thou the Lord of all things, Who standest in need of no one, hast been pleased by this Sacrament to dwell in us.

Preserve my heart and my body without stain, that with a joyful and clean conscience I may be able often to celebrate Thy sacred mysteries, and to receive for my eternal salvation what Thou hast principally ordained and instituted for Thine honour and perpetual remembrance.

6. Rejoice, O my soul, and give thanks to thy God for so noble a gift, and so singular a comfort left to thee in this vale of tears.

For as often as thou repeatest this mystery, and receivest the Body of Christ, so often dost thou celebrate the work of thy redemption, and art made partaker of all the merits of Christ.

For the charity of Christ is never diminished, and the greatness of His propitiation is never exhausted.

Therefore oughtest thou to dispose thyself for this, by perpetually renewing the vigour of thy mind, and to weigh with attentive consideration this great mystery of thy salvation.

And as often as thou sayest or hearest Mass, it ought to seem to thee as great, new, and delightful as if Christ that same day, first descending into the Virgin's womb, had been made man; or hanging on the cross, was suffering and dying for the salvation of mankind.

CHAPTER III

On Frequent Communion

DISCIPLE

BEHOLD, I come to Thee, O Lord, that it may be well with me by Thy gift, and that I may be delighted in Thy holy banquet, which "in Thy sweetness, O God, thou hast provided for the poor." (Ps. 67:11).

Behold, in Thee is all whatsoever I can or ought to desire; Thou art my salvation and redemption, my hope and my strength, my honour and my glory.

Therefore, "Give joy to the soul of thy servant, for to thee, this day, O Lord Jesus, I have lifted up my soul." (Ps. 85:4).

I desire at this time to receive Thee devoutly and reverently; I would gladly bring Thee into my house, that, like Zacheus, I may receive Thy blessing, and be numbered among the children of Abraham. (Luke 19:9).

My soul longs to be nourished with Thy Body; my heart desires to be united with Thee.

2. Give Thyself to me and it is enough; for without Thee no comfort is available.

Without Thee I cannot subsist; and without Thy visitation I cannot live.

And, therefore, I must come often to Thee, and receive Thee for the remedy, and for the health and strength of my soul; lest perhaps I faint in the way, if I be deprived of this heavenly food.

For so, O most merciful Jesus, Thou wast pleased once to say, when Thou hadst been preaching to the people, and curing sundry diseases: "I will not send them away fasting, lest they faint in the way." (Matt. 15:32).

Deal now in like manner with me, Who hast left Thyself in the Sacrament for the comfort of Thy faithful.

For Thou art the most sweet refection of the soul; and he that shall eat Thee worthily shall be partaker and heir of everlasting glory.

It is indeed necessary for me, who so often fall and commit sin, and so quickly grow slack and faint, by frequent prayers and confessions, and by the holy communion of Thy Body, to repair my strength, to cleanse and inflame my soul, lest perhaps by abstaining for a longer time, I fall away from my holy purpose.

3. For the imaginations of man are prone to evil from his youth (Gen. 8:21); and unless Thy divine medicine succour him man quickly becomes worse.

The Holy Communion, therefore, withdraws him from evil, and strengthens him in good.

But if I am so often negligent and lukewarm now when I communicate, or celebrate, how would it be were I not to take this remedy, and seek so great a help?

And although I am not every day fit nor well disposed to celebrate, yet I will endeavour, at proper times, to receive the divine mysteries, and to make myself partaker of so great a grace.

For this is the one main comfort of a faithful soul, so long as she sojourns afar off from Thee in this mortal body; being mindful often of her God, to receive her beloved with a devout mind.

4. O wonderful condescension of Thy tender love towards us, that Thou, O Lord God, the Creator and enlivener of all

spirits, shouldst vouchsafe to come to a poor soul, and with Thy whole divinity and humanity, satisfy her hunger!

O happy mind, and blessed soul, which deserves to receive Thee, her Lord God, devoutly; and in receiving Thee, to be filled with spiritual joy!

Oh, how great a lord does she entertain! how beloved a guest does she bring into her house! how sweet a companion does she receive! how faithful a friend does she accept of! how beautiful and how noble a spouse does she embrace, beloved above all, and to be loved beyond all that she can desire!

Let Heaven and earth, with all their attire, be silent in Thy presence, O my dearest beloved (Hab. 2:20); for whatever praise or beauty they have is all the gift of Thy bounty; nor can they equal the beauty of Thy name, of whose wisdom there is no end.

CHAPTER IV
Benefits to Devout Communicants

Disciple

O LORD, my God, anticipate Thy servant with blessings of Thy sweetness (Ps. 20:4), that I may approach worthily and devoutly to Thy magnificent Sacrament.

Raise up my heart towards Thee, and deliver me from this heavy sluggishness. Visit me with Thy grace, that I may taste in spirit Thy sweetness (Ps. 33:9), which plentifully lies hid in this Sacrament (Apoc. 2:17), as in its fountain.

Illuminate also my eyes (Ps. 12:4), to behold so great a mystery, and strengthen me to believe it with an undoubting faith.

For it is Thy work, not the power of man; Thy sacred institution, not man's invention.

For no man can be found able of himself to know and understand these things, which surpass even the subtlety of angels.

What shall I, therefore, an unworthy sinner, who am but dust and ashes (Gen. 18:27), be able to search into or conceive of so high and sacred a mystery?

2. O Lord, in the simplicity of my heart, with a good and firm faith, and in obedience to Thy command, I come to Thee with hope and reverence; and I do verily believe that Thou art here present in the Sacrament, God and man.

It is then Thy will that I should receive Thee, and through love unite myself to Thee.

Wherefore, I implore Thy mercy; and I beg of Thee to give me for this a special grace, that I may be wholly melted away in Thee and overflow with Thy love, and never more seek comfort in aught else.

For this most high and most excellent Sacrament is the health of soul and body, the remedy of all spiritual diseases, by which my vices are cured, my passions are restrained, temptations are overcome or lessened, a greater grace is infused, virtue receives an increase, faith is confirmed, hope strengthened, and charity inflamed and extended.

3. For Thou hast bestowed, and still often times dost bestow, many good things in this Sacrament on Thy beloved, who communicate devoutly, O my God, Thou support of my soul, Who art the repairer of human infirmity, and the giver of all interior consolations.

For Thou impartest unto them much consolation to support them in their many troubles; and Thou liftest them up from the depth of their own dejection to the hope of Thy protection; and Thou dost recreate and enlighten them interiorly with a certain new grace, so that they who before communion were anxious, and felt no affection in themselves, after being fed with this heavenly meat and drink, find themselves changed for the better.

And Thou art pleased thus to deal with Thine elect, to the end that they may truly acknowledge and plainly experience how great is their infirmity when left to themselves, and how much they receive from Thy bounty and grace.

For of themselves they are cold, dry, and in-devout; but by Thee they are made fervent, cheerful, and devout.

For who is he that, approaching humbly to the fountain of sweetness, does not carry away with him some little sweetness?

Or who, standing by a great fire, does not receive from it some little heat?

Now, Thou art the fountain always full and overflowing; Thou art a fire always burning and never decaying. (John 4:14; Heb. 12:29).

4. Wherefore, if I cannot draw out of the fullness of the fountain, nor drink my fill, I will at least set my mouth to the orifice of this heavenly pipe, that so I may draw from it some small drop to refresh my thirst, to the end that I may not wholly be dried up.

And if I cannot as yet be all heavenly, and all on fire, like the cherubim and seraphim, I will, however, endeavour to apply myself to devotion, and to prepare my heart for acquiring some small flame of divine fire, by humbly receiving this life-giving Sacrament.

And whatever is wanting to me, O good Jesus, most blessed Saviour, do Thou in Thy bounty and goodness supply for me, Who hast vouchsafed to call all unto Thee, saying, "Come to Me, all you that labour and are burdened, and I will refresh you."

I labour indeed in the sweat of my brow, I am tormented with grief of heart, I am burdened with sins, I am troubled with temptations, and am entangled and oppressed with many evil passions; and there is no one to help me (Ps. 21:12), no one to deliver and save me, but Thou, O Lord God, my Saviour (Ps. 24:5), to Whom I commit myself and all that is mine, that Thou mayest keep me, and bring me to everlasting life.

Receive me for the praise and glory of Thy name, Who hast prepared Thy Body and Blood for my meat and drink.

Grant, O Lord God, my Saviour, that with the frequenting of this Thy mystery, the affection of my devotion may increase.

CHAPTER V

Dignity of the Sacrament

Christ

IF thou hadst the purity of an angel, and the sanctity of St. John the Baptist, thou wouldst not be worthy to receive or handle the Sacrament.

For this is not due to any merits of men, that a man should consecrate and handle the Sacrament of Christ, and receive for his food the bread of angels. (Ps. 77:25).

Great is this mystery, and great the dignity of priests, to whom that is given which is not granted to angels.

For priests alone, rightly ordained in the Church, have power to celebrate and to consecrate the Body of Christ.

The priest indeed is the minister of God, using the word of God, and by the command and institution of God: but God Himself is there, the principal author and invisible worker, to whom is subject all that He wills, and to whose command everything is obedient.

2. Thou must, therefore, give more credit to an omnipotent God, in everything relating to this most excellent Sacrament, than to thine own sense or any visible sign; and, therefore, thou art to approach to this work with fear and reverence.

Take heed to thyself (7 Tim. 4:16) and see what kind of ministry has been delivered to thee by the imposition of the bishop's hands.

Lo! thou art made a priest, and art consecrated to say Mass; see now that in due time thou faithfully and devoutly offer up sacrifice to God, and that thou behave thyself in such manner as to be without reproof.

Thou hast not lightened thy burden, but art now bound with a stricter band of discipline, and art obliged to a greater perfection of sanctity.

A priest ought to be adorned with all virtues, and to give example of a good life to others. (Titus 2:7).

His conversation should not be with the ordinary and common ways of men but with the angels in Heaven (Phil. 3:20), or with perfect men upon earth.

3. A priest clad in his sacred vestments is Christ's vicegerent, to pray to God for himself, and for all the people, in a suppliant and humble manner.

He has before him and behind him the sign of the cross of the Lord that he may always remember the passion of Christ.

He bears the cross before him in his vestment that he may diligently behold the footsteps of Christ, and fervently endeavour to follow them.

He is marked with the cross behind that he may mildly suffer, for God's sake, whatsoever adversities shall befall him from others.

He wears the cross before him that he may bewail his own sins; behind him, that through compassion he may lament the sins of others, and know that he is placed, as it were a mediator between God and the sinner. Neither ought he to cease from prayer and holy oblation until he be favoured with the grace and mercy which he implores.

When a priest celebrates he honours God, he rejoices the angels, he edifies the Church, he helps the living, he obtains rest for the dead, and makes himself partaker of all that is good.

CHAPTER VI

A Petition Before Communion

DISCIPLE

WHEN I consider Thy greatness, O Lord, and my own vileness, I tremble very much, and am confounded in myself.

For if I come not to Thee I fly from life; and if I intrude myself unworthily I incur Thy displeasure.

What then shall I do, O my God, my helper, my counsellor in necessities?

2. Do Thou teach me the right way: appoint me some short exercise proper for the Holy Communion.

For it is necessary to know in what manner I should reverently and devoutly prepare my heart for Thee, for the profitable receiving of Thy Sacrament, or for celebrating so great and divine a sacrifice.

CHAPTER VII

Resolution of Amendment

CHRIST

ABOVE all things it behooves the priest of God to come to the celebrating, handling, and receiving this Sacrament with very great humility of heart, and lowly reverence; with an entire faith, and a pious intention of the honour of God.

Diligently examine thy conscience, and to the best of thy power cleanse and purify it by true contrition and humble confession: so that there be nothing weighty to give thee remorse and hinder thy free access.

Repent thee of all thy sins in general, and in particular lament and grieve for thy daily offences.

And if thou hast time confess to thy God, in the secret of thy heart, all the miseries of thy passions.

2. Sigh and grieve that thou art yet so carnal and worldly, so unmortified in thy passions, so full of the motions of concupiscence;

So unguarded in thine outward senses, so often entangled with many vain imaginations;

So much inclined to exterior things, so negligent as to the interior;

So easy to laughter and dissipation, so hard to tears and compunction;

So prone to relaxation and to the pleasures of the flesh, so sluggish to austerity and fervour;

So curious to hear news, and to see fine sights, so remiss to embrace things humble and abject;

So covetous to possess much, so sparing in giving, so close in retaining;

So inconsiderate in speech, so little able to hold thy peace;

So disorderly in thy carriage, so over-eager in thine actions;

So greedy at meat, so deaf to the word of God;

So hasty for rest, so slow to labour;

So wakeful to hear idle tales, so drowsy to watch in the service of God;

So hasty to make an end of thy prayers, so wandering as to attention;

So negligent in saying thine office, so tepid in celebrating, so dry at the time of receiving;

So quickly distracted, so seldom quite recollected within thyself;

So easily moved to anger, so apt to take offence at others;

So prone to judge, so severe in reprehending;

So joyful in prosperity, so weak in adversity;

So often proposing many good things, and effecting little.

3. Having confessed and bewailed these and thine other defects with sorrow and a great dislike of thine own weakness, make a strong resolution always to amend thy life and to advance in virtue.

Then with a full resignation and with thy whole will, offer thyself up to the honour of My name, on the altar of thy heart, as a perpetual holocaust, by committing faithfully to Me both thy soul and body.

That so thou mayest be worthy to approach to offer up sacrifice to God, and to receive for thy salvation the Sacrament of My Body.

4. For there is no oblation more worthy, nor satisfaction greater for washing away sins, than with the oblation of the Body of Christ, in the Mass and in the Communion, to offer up thy self purely and entirely to God.

If a man does what lies in him, and is truly penitent, as often as he shall come to Me for pardon and grace, "As I live, saith the Lord God, I desire not the death of the sinner, but that he should be converted from his ways and live" (Ezech. 33:11; 18:23), I will no longer remember his iniquities (Ibid. 22), but all shall be forgiven him.

CHAPTER VIII
The Oblation of Christ

CHRIST

AS I willingly offered myself to God My Father, for thy sins, with My hands stretched out upon the cross, and My body naked, so that nothing remained in Me which was not turned into a sacrifice, to appease the divine wrath:

Even so must thou willingly offer thyself to Me daily in the Mass, for a pure and holy oblation, together with all thy powers and affections, as heartily as thou art able.

What do I require more of thee, than that thou endeavour to resign thyself entirely to Me?

Whatsoever thou givest besides thyself I regard not; for I seek not thy gift, but thyself.

2. As it would not suffice thee if thou hadst all things but Me, so neither can it please Me whatever thou givest, as long as thou offerest not thyself.

Offer thyself to Me, and give thy whole self for God, and thine offering will be accepted.

Behold, I offered My whole self to the Father for thee, and have given My whole Body and Blood for thy food, that I might be all thine, and thou mightest be always Mine.

But if thou wilt stand upon thine own self, and wilt not offer thyself freely to My will, thine offering is not perfect, nor will there be an entire union between us.

Therefore, before all thy works, thou must make a free oblation of thyself into the hands of God, if thou desire to obtain liberty and grace.

For the reason why so few become illuminated and internally free is because they do not wholly renounce themselves.

My sentence stands firm: "Unless a man renounce all he cannot be my disciple." (Luke 14:33). If, therefore, thou desire to be My disciple, offer up thyself to Me with all thine affections.

CHAPTER IX
An Offering to God

Disciple

LORD, all things are Thine that are in Heaven and earth.

I desire to offer myself up to Thee as a voluntary oblation, and to remain forever Thine.

Lord, in the sincerity of my heart I offer myself to Thee this day to be Thy servant evermore, to serve Thee, and to become a sacrifice of perpetual praise to Thee.

Receive me with this sacred oblation of Thy precious Body, which I offer to Thee this day, in the presence of Thine angels invisibly standing by, that it may be for mine and all the people's salvation.

2. Lord, I offer to Thee all my sins and offences which I have committed in Thy sight and that of Thy holy angels, from the day that I was first capable of sin until this hour, upon Thy propitiatory altar, that Thou mayest burn and consume them all with the fire of Thy charity, and remove all the stains of my sins, and cleanse my conscience from all offences, and restore to me Thy grace, which I have lost by sin, by fully pardoning me all, and mercifully receiving me to the kiss of peace. (Heb. 9:13, 14).

3. What can I do for my sins but humbly confess, them, and lament them, and incessantly implore Thy mercy for them.

Hear me, I beseech Thee, in Thy mercy, where I stand before Thee, O my God.

All my sins displease me exceedingly, I will never commit them anymore; I am sorry for them, and will be sorry for them as long as I live; I am willing to do penance for them, and to make satisfaction to the utmost of my power.

Forgive, O my God, forgive me my sins for Thy holy name's sake; save my soul, which Thou hast redeemed with Thy precious Blood. (7 Ptr. 1:19).

Behold, I commit myself to Thy mercy; I resign myself into Thy hands.

Deal with me according to Thy goodness (Ps. 118:124), not according to my wickedness and iniquity. (Ps. 102:10).

I offer also to Thee all the good I have, though very little and imperfect; that Thou mayest make it better and sanctify it; that Thou mayest be pleased with it, and make it acceptable to Thee, and perfect it more and more; and mayest moreover bring me, who am a slothful and unprofitable wretch, to a good and happy end.

I offer to Thee also all the godly desires of Thy devout servants, the necessities of my parents, friends, brethren, sisters, and all of those that are dear to me; and of all such as, for the love of Thee, have been benefactors to me or others; or who have desired and begged of me to offer up prayers and Masses for themselves and all that belonged to them; whether they live as yet in the flesh, or whether they are now departed out of this world!

That they all may be sensible of the assistance of Thy grace, of the benefit of Thy comfort, of Thy protection from dangers, and of a deliverance from their pains, and that being freed from all evils they may with joy give worthy thanks to Thee.

6. I offer up also to Thee my prayers and this sacrifice of propitiation for those in particular who have in anything wronged, grieved, or abused me, or have done me any damage or displeasure.

And for all those likewise whom I have at any time grieved, troubled, injured, or scandalized, by word or deed, knowingly or unknowingly; that it may please Thee to forgive us all our sins and offences one against another.

Take, O Lord, from our hearts all jealousy, indignation, wrath, and contention, and whatsoever may hurt charity, and lessen brotherly love.

Have mercy, O Lord, have mercy on those that crave Thy mercy; give grace to them that stand in need thereof, and grant that we may be worthy to enjoy Thy grace, and that we may attain to life everlasting. Amen.

CHAPTER X
The Holy Communion

CHRIST

THOU oughtest often to have recourse to the fountain of grace, and of divine mercy, to the fountain of all goodness and all purity, that thou mayest be healed of thy passions and vices, and be made more strong and vigilant against all the temptations and deceits of the devil.

The enemy, knowing the very great advantage and remedy which is in the Holy Communion, strives by all means and occasions, as much as he is able, to withdraw and hinder faithful and devout persons from it.

2. For when some are preparing themselves for the sacred Communion, they suffer the greater assaults of Satan.

This wicked spirit, as it is written in Job (1:6), cometh amongst the sons of God, to trouble them with his accustomed malice, or to make them overfearful and perplexed, that so he may diminish their devotion, or, by his assaults, take away their faith: so that perhaps, they may altogether omit the Communion, or at least approach it with tepidity.

But there is no regard to be paid to his wiles and suggestions, be they ever so filthy and abominable; but all his attempts are to be turned back upon his own head.

The wretch is to be condemned and scorned, nor is the Holy Communion to be omitted for his assaults, and the commotions which he causes.

3. Oftentimes also a person is hindered by too great a solicitude for obtaining devotion, and a certain anxiety about making his confession.

Follow herein the counsel of the wise, and put away all anxiety and scruple, for it hindereth the grace of God, and destroyeth devotion.

Leave not the Holy Communion for every small trouble and vexation, but go quickly to confession, and willingly forgive others their offenses against thee.

And if thou hast offended anyone, humbly crave pardon, and God will readily forgive thee.

4. What doth it avail thee to delay thy confession for a long time, or to put off the Holy Communion?

Purge thyself with speed, spit out the venom presently, make haste to take this remedy, and thou shalt find it to be better for thee than if thou hadst deferred it for a long time.

If thou deferrest it today, for this cause, perhaps tomorrow a greater will occur and so thou mayest be hindered a long time from Communion, and become more unfit.

With all possible speed shake off this heaviness and sloth, for it is to no purpose to continue long in uneasiness, to pass a long time in trouble, and for these daily impediments to withdraw thyself from the divine mysteries.

Yea, it is very hurtful to delay the Communion long; for this usually causeth a great lukewarmness and numbness.

Alas! some tepid and dissolute people are willing to put off their confession, and desire that their Communion should be deferred, lest they should be obliged thereby to keep a strict watch over themselves.

Ah! how little is their love of God; how weak is their devotion, who so easily put off the sacred Communion!

How happy is he, and acceptable to God, who so liveth, and keepeth his conscience in such purity, as to be ready and well disposed to communicate every day, if it were permitted, and he might do it without being singular.

If sometimes a person abstains out of humility, or by reason of some lawful impediment, he is to be commended for his reverence.

But if sloth steal upon him, he must stir up himself, and do what lieth in him; and God will assist his desire for his good will, which He chiefly regards.

7. And when he is lawfully hindered, he must yet always have a good will and pious intentions to communicate, and so he shall not lose the fruit of the Sacrament.

For every devout man may every day, and every hour, receive Christ spiritually without any prohibition, and with great profit to his soul.

And yet on certain days, and at the times appointed, he ought, with an affectionate reverence, to receive sacramentally the Body of his Redeemer, and rather aim at the praise and honour of God than seek his own comfort.

For he communicates mystically, and is invisibly fed, as often as he devoutly calleth to mind the mystery of the Incarnation and Passion of Christ, and is inflamed with the love of Him.

8. He that prepareth not himself but when a festival draweth near, or when custom compelleth him thereunto, shall often be unprepared.

Blessed is he that offereth himself up as a holocaust to the Lord as often as he celebrates or communicates.

Be neither too long nor too hasty in celebrating, but observe the good common manner of those with whom thou livest.

Thou oughtest not to be too tedious and troublesome to others, but to keep the common way according to the appointment of superiors, and rather consult the profit of others than thine own inclination or devotion.

CHAPTER XI
The Body of Christ

DISCIPLE

O SWEETEST Lord Jesus, what great sweetness hath a devout soul that feasteth with Thee in Thy banquet; where there is no other meat set before her to be eaten but Thyself, her only beloved, and most to be desired, above all the desires of her heart.

And to me indeed it would be delightful to pour out tears in Thy presence, with the whole affection of my heart, and like the devout Magdalen to wash Thy feet with my tears. (Luke 7:38).

But where is this devotion, where is this plentiful shedding of holy tears?

Surely in the sight of Thee, and of Thy holy angels, my whole heart ought to be inflamed and to weep for joy.

For I have Thee in the Sacrament truly present, though hidden under another form.

2. For to behold Thee in Thine own divine brightness is what mine eyes would not be able to endure, neither could the whole world subsist in the splendour of the glory of Thy majesty.

In this, therefore, Thou condescendest to my weakness, that Thou hidest Thyself under the Sacrament.

I truly have and adore Him whom the angels adore in Heaven; but I as yet in faith, they by sight, and without a veil. (1 Cor. 13:12).

I must be content with the light of true faith, and walk therein till the day of eternal brightness breaks forth, and the shades of figures pass away. (Cant. 2:17).

But when that which is perfect shall come (1 Cor. 13:10), the use of Sacraments shall cease; for the blessed in heavenly glory stand not in need of the medicine of the Sacraments.

For they rejoice without end in the presence of God, beholding His glory face to face (1 Cor. 13:12): and being transformed from glory into the glory (2 Cor. 3:18) of the incomprehensible Deity, they taste the Word of God made flesh (John 1:14), as He was from the beginning, and as He remaineth forever.

3. When I call to mind these wonders, even every spiritual comfort becomes grievously tedious to me; because as long as I behold not my Lord openly in His glory I make no account of anything I see and hear in the world.

Thou art my witness, O God, that not one thing can comfort me, nor anything created give me rest, but only Thou, my God, whom I desire forever to contemplate.

But this is not possible whilst I remain in this mortal life.

And, therefore, I must endeavour to acquire much patience and submit myself to Thee in all my desires.

For Thy saints also, O Lord, who now rejoice with Thee in the Kingdom of Heaven, whilst they were living expected in faith and great patience the coming of Thy glory. What they believed I believe; what they hoped for I hope for; and whither they are gone I trust that I also, through Thy grace, shall go.

In the meantime I will walk in faith (2 Cor. 5:7), strengthened by the examples of Thy saints.

I shall have moreover for my comfort, and the direction of my life, the holy books (1 Mach. 12:9); and above all these things Thy most holy Body for a singular remedy and refuge.

4. For in this life I find there are two things especially necessary for me, without which this miserable life would be insupportable.

Whilst I am kept in the prison of this body I acknowledge myself to need two things, namely, food and light.

Thou hast therefore given to me, weak as I am, Thy sacred Body, for the nourishment of my soul and body, and Thou hast set "thy word as a lamp to my feet." (Ps. 118:105).

Without these two I could not well live, for the word of God is the light of my soul and Thy Sacrament is the bread of life. (John 6:35).

These also may be called the two tables set on either side in the storehouse of Thy holy Church.

One is the table of the holy altar having the holy bread, that is, the precious Body of Christ;

The other is that of the divine law, containing Thy holy doctrine, teaching the right faith, and firmly leading even within the veil, where is the holy of holies.

Thanks be to Thee, O Lord Jesus, Light of eternal Light, for the table of holy doctrine which Thou hast afforded us by the ministry of Thy servants, the Prophets and Apostles, and other teachers.

Thanks be to Thee, O Thou Creator and Redeemer of men, Who to manifest Thy love to the whole world hast prepared a great supper (Luke 14:16), wherein Thou hast set before us to be eaten, not the typical lamb, but Thy most sacred Body and Blood; rejoicing all the faithful with Thy holy banquet, and inebriating them with the cup of salvation (Ps. 22:5), in which are all the delights of Paradise; and the holy angels feast with us, but with a more happy sweetness.

Oh, how great and honourable is the office of priests, to whom it is given to consecrate with sacred words the Lord of majesty; to bless Him with their lips, to hold Him with their hands, to receive Him with their own mouths, and to administer Him to others!

Oh! how clean ought those hands to be, how pure that mouth, how holy that body, how unspotted the heart of a priest, into whom the Author of purity so often enters.

From the mouth of a priest nothing but what is holy, no word but what is good and profitable ought to proceed, who so often receives the Sacrament of Christ.

7. His eyes ought to be simple and chaste, which are used to behold the Body of Christ: his hands pure and lifted up to Heaven, which are used to handle the Creator of Heaven and earth.

Unto the priests especially it is said in the law: Be ye holy, because I the Lord your God am holy. (Lev. 19:2).

8. Let Thy grace, O Almighty God, assist us, that we, who have undertaken the office of priesthood, may serve Thee worthily and devoutly in all purity and good conscience. (1 Tim. 1:5).

And if we cannot live in such great innocence as we ought, grant us at least duly to bewail the sins which we have committed; and in the spirit of humility, and the resolution of a good will, to serve Thee more fervently for the time to come.

CHAPTER XII

Preparation for Communion

CHRIST

I AM the lover of purity and the giver of all holiness. I seek a pure heart, and there is the place of My rest. (Is. 66:1).

Make ready for Me "a large upper room furnished, and I will eat the pasch with thee, together with My disciples." (Mark 14:14, 15).

If thou wilt have Me come to thee, and remain with thee, purge out the old leaven (1 Cor. 5:7), and make clean the habitation of thy heart.

Shut out the whole world, and all the tumult of vices: sit like a sparrow solitary on the housetop (Ps. 101:8), and think of thine excesses in the bitterness of thy soul. (Is. 38:15).

For every lover prepareth the best and fairest room for his dearly beloved; and hereby is known the affection of him that entertaineth his beloved.

2. Know, nevertheless, that thou canst not sufficiently prepare thyself by the merit of any action of thine although thou shouldst prepare thyself a whole year together, and think of nothing else.

But it is of My mere goodness and grace that thou art suffered to come to My table; as if a beggar should be invited to dinner by a rich man, who hath nothing else to return him for his benefits but to humble himself and give him thanks.

Do what lieth in thee, and do it diligently; not out of custom, nor for necessity, but with fear, reverence, and affection, receive the Body of thy beloved Lord, thy God, who vouchsafes to come to thee.

I am He that hath invited thee, I have commanded it to be done, I will supply what is wanting in thee; come and receive Me.

3. When I bestow the grace of devotion give thanks to thy God, not for that thou art worthy, but because I have had mercy on thee. (Luke 18:10, 13).

If thou hast it not, but rather findest thyself dry, continue in prayer, sigh and knock at the gate of divine mercy; and give not over till thou receive some crumb or drop of divine grace.

Thou hast need of Me, not I of thee.

Neither dost thou come to sanctify Me, but I come to sanctify and make thee better.

Thou comest that thou mayest be sanctified by Me, and united to Me; that thou mayest receive new grace, and be inflamed anew to amendment.

Neglect not this grace, but prepare thy heart with all diligence, and bring thy beloved into thy heart.

4. But thou oughtest not only to prepare thy self by devotion before Communion, but care fully also to keep thyself therein after receiving the Sacrament; neither is carefully guarding thy self afterwards less required than devoutly preparing thyself before; for a good guard afterwards is the best preparation for again obtaining greater grace.

For what renders a man very much indisposed is presently turning himself to seek exterior consolation.

Beware of much talk, remain in secret and enjoy thy God; for thou hast Him whom all the world cannot take from thee.

I am He to whom thou oughtest to give thy whole self; so that thou mayest henceforward live, without any solicitude, not in thyself but in Me. (Gal. 2:20).

CHAPTER XIII
Desires of a Devout Soul

DISCIPLE

WHO will give me, O Lord, that I may find Thee alone, that I may open my whole heart to Thee and enjoy Thee as my soul desireth; and that now no man may despise me (Cant. 8:1), nor anything created move me or regard me, but that Thou alone speak to me, and I to Thee; as the beloved is wont to speak to his beloved, and a friend to entertain himself with his friend. (Ex. 33:11).

This I pray for, this I desire, that I may be wholly united to Thee, and may withdraw my heart from all created things, and by the Holy Communion, and often celebrating, may more and more learn to relish heavenly and eternal things.

Ah! Lord God, when shall I be wholly united to Thee, and absorbed in Thee, and altogether forgetful of myself?

Thou in me, and I in Thee; and so grant us both to continue in one. (John 15:5).

2. Verily Thou art my beloved, the choicest amongst thousands (Cant. 5:10), in whom my soul is well pleased to dwell all the days of her life.

Verily Thou art my peacemaker (Cant. 8:10), in Whom is sovereign peace and true rest; out of Whom is labour and sorrow and endless misery.

Thou art, in truth, a hidden God (Is. 45:15), and Thy counsel is not with the wicked; but Thy conversation is with the humble and the simple. (Prov. 3:32).

Oh, how sweet is Thy spirit, O Lord, Who, to show Thy sweetness towards Thy children, vouchsafest to feed them with the most delicious bread which cometh down from Heaven! (John 6:50).

Surely, there is no other nation so great, that hath gods so nigh them as Thou our God art present (Deut. 4:7) to all Thy faithful; to whom, for their daily comfort, and for the raising up of their hearts to Heaven, Thou givest Thyself to be eaten and enjoyed.

3. For what other nation is there so honoured as the Christian people?

Or what creature under Heaven so beloved as a devout soul, into whom God cometh, that He may feed her with His glorious Flesh?

O unspeakable grace! O wonderful condescension! O infinite love, singularly bestowed upon man!

But what return shall I make to the Lord for this grace, and for so extraordinary a charity? (Ps. 115:12).

There is nothing that I can give Him that will please Him better than if I give up my heart entirely to God, and unite it closely to Him. (Prov. 23:26).

Then all that is within me shall rejoice exceedingly when my soul shall be perfectly united to my God; then will He say to me: If thou wilt be with Me, I will be with thee: and I will answer Him: Vouchsafe, O Lord, to remain with me, and I will willingly be with Thee.

This is my whole desire, that my heart may be united to Thee.

CHAPTER XIV

Desire to Receive Jesus

DISCIPLE

OH, how great is the multitude of Thy sweetness, O Lord, which Thou hast hidden for them that fear Thee! (Ps. 30:20). When I remember some devout persons, who came to Thy Sacrament with the greatest devotion and affection, I am often confounded and ashamed within myself, that I approach so tepidly and coldly to Thine altar, and to the table of the Holy Communion; that I remain so dry, and without affection of heart; that I am not wholly set on fire in Thy presence, O my God, nor so earnestly drawn and affected, as many devout persons have been, who, out of a vehement desire of communion, and a sensible love in their hearts, could not contain themselves from weeping; but with their whole souls eagerly thirsted to approach, both with the mouth of their heart and their body, to Thee, O God, the living fountain; being in nowise able to moderate or satisfy their hunger, but by receiving Thy Body with all joy and spiritual eagerness. (Ps. 41:3).

2. O true ardent faith of these persons, being a probable argument of Thy sacred presence!

For they truly know their Lord in the breaking of bread, whose heart burneth so mightily within them, from Jesus walking with them. (Luke 24:35).

Such affection and devotion as this, so vehement a love and burning, is often far from me.

Be Thou merciful to me, O good Jesus, sweet and gracious Lord, and grant me, Thy poor suppliant, to feel sometimes at least, in the sacred Communion, some little of the cordial affection of Thy love, that my faith may be more strengthened, my hope in Thy goodness increased, and that my charity, being once perfectly enkindled, and having tasted the manna of Heaven, may never decay. (2 Cor. 9:8).

3. Moreover, Thy mercy is able to give me the grace I desire, and to visit me in Thy great clemency with the spirit of fervour, when it shall please Thee:

For though I burn not at present with so great a desire as those that are so singularly devoted to Thee; yet, by Thy grace, I desire to have this same greatly inflamed desire; praying and wishing that I may be made partaker with all such Thy fervent lovers and be numbered in their holy company.

CHAPTER XV
Humility and Self-Denial

CHRIST

T'HOU oughtest to seek the grace of devotion earnestly, to ask it fervently, to wait for it patiently and confidently, to receive it thankfully, to keep it humbly, to work with it diligently, and to commit to God the time and manner of heavenly visitation, until it please Him to come unto thee.

Thou oughtest chiefly to humble thyself when thou feelest inwardly little or no devotion; and yet not to be too much dejected, nor to grieve inordinately.

God often giveth in one short moment what He hath a long time denied.

He giveth sometimes in the end that which in the beginning of prayer He deferred to grant.

2. If grace were always presently given, and ever at hand with a wish, it would be more than man's infirmity could well bear.

Therefore the grace of devotion is to be expected with a good hope and humble patience. Yet impute it to thyself and to thy sins, when it is not given thee, or when it is secretly taken away.

It is sometimes a little thing that hinders or hides grace from thee; if that may be called a little, and not rather great, which hindereth so great a good.

But if thou remove this same, be it small or great, and perfectly overcome it, thou shalt have thy desire.

3. For as soon as ever thou hast delivered thy self up to God with thy whole heart, and neither seekest this nor that for thine own pleasure or will, but wholly placest thyself in Him, thou shalt find thyself united to Him, and at peace; for nothing will relish so well and please thee so much as the good pleasure of the divine will.

Whosoever, therefore, with a single heart shall direct his attention upwards to God, and purify himself from all inordinate love or dislike of any created thing, shall be the most fit to receive grace, and worthy of the gift of devotion. (Matt. 6:22).

For the Lord bestows His blessing there where He finds the vessels empty.

And the more perfectly one forsakes these things below, and the more he dies to himself by the contempt of himself, the more speedily grace cometh, entereth in more plentifully, and the higher it elevateth the free heart.

4. "Then shall he see and abound; his heart shall wonder and be enlarged" (Is. 60:5) within him, because the hand of the Lord is with him, and he has put himself wholly into His hand forever. Behold, thus shall the man be blessed that seeketh God with his whole heart, and taketh not his soul in vain.

Such a one as this, in receiving the Holy Eucharist, obtains a great grace of divine union, because he looks not towards his own devotion and comfort, but, above all devotion and comfort, regards the honour and glory of God.

CHAPTER XVI
Laying Open Our Necessities

DISCIPLE

O MOST sweet and loving Lord, whom I now desire to receive with all devotion, Thou knowest my weakness and the necessity which I endure; in what great evils and vices I am immersed; how often I am oppressed, tempted, troubled, and defiled. (Ps. 138:16).

To Thee I come for remedy; I pray to Thee for comfort and succour.

I speak to Him that knows all things, to whom all that is within me is manifest, and who alone can perfectly comfort and help me.

Thou knowest what good things I stand most in need of, and how poor I am in virtues.

2. Behold, I stand before Thee poor and naked, begging Thy grace, and imploring Thy mercy.

Feed Thy hungry suppliant, inflame my coldness with the fire of Thy love, enlighten my blindness with the brightness of Thy presence.

Teach me to look upon all earthly things with disgust, to

bear all things grievous and afflicting with patience, and to look upon all things created with contempt and disregard.

Lift up my heart to Thee in Heaven, and suffer me not to wander upon earth.

Be Thou only sweet to me from henceforth forevermore; for Thou only art my meat and drink, my love and my joy, my sweetness and all my good.

3. Oh, that with Thy presence Thou wouldst inflame, burn, and transform me into Thyself, that I may be made one spirit with Thee, by the grace of eternal union, and by the melting of ardent love.

Suffer me not to go from Thee hungry and thirsty, but deal with me in Thy mercy as Thou hast often dealt wonderfully with Thy saints.

What marvel if I should be wholly set on fire by Thee, and should die to myself; since Thou art a fire always burning (Heb. 12:29), and never decaying; a love purifying the hearts and enlightening the understanding.

CHAPTER XVII
Desire to Serve Christ

DISCIPLE

WITH the greatest devotion and burning love, with all the affection and fervour of my heart, I desire to receive Thee, O Lord; as many saints and devout persons, who were most pleasing to Thee by holiness of life, and most fervent devotion, have desired Thee, when they communicated.

O my God, my eternal love, my whole good, and neverending happiness, I would gladly receive Thee with the most vehement desire, and most worthy reverence, that any of the saints have ever had or could experience.

2. And although I am unworthy to have all those feelings of

devotion, yet I offer to Thee the whole affection of my heart, as if I alone had all those highly pleasing and inflamed desires.

Yea, and whatsoever a godly mind can conceive and desire, all this with the greatest reverence and most inward affection, I offer and present to Thee.

I desire to reserve nothing to myself, but freely and most willingly to sacrifice myself, and all that is mine, to Thee.

O Lord, my God, my Creator, and my Redeemer, I desire to receive Thee this day with such affection, reverence, praise, and honour; with such gratitude, worthiness, and love; with such faith, hope, and purity, as Thy most holy Mother, the glorious Virgin Mary, received and desired Thee, when she humbly and devoutly answered the angel, who declared to her the mystery of the Incarnation, saying: "Behold the handmaid of the Lord; be it done to me according to thy word." (Luke 1:38).

3. And as Thy blessed forerunner, the most excellent among the saints, John the Baptist, in Thy presence leaped for joy through the Holy Ghost, while he was yet shut up in his mother's womb, and afterwards seeing Jesus walking amongst men, humbling himself exceedingly, said, with devout affection: "The friend of the bridegroom, who standeth and heareth him, rejoiceth with joy because of the bridegroom's voice." (John 3:29). So I also wish to be inflamed with great and holy desires, and to present myself to Thee with my whole heart.

Wherefore I here offer and present to Thee the excessive joys of all devout hearts, their ardent affections, their ecstasies and supernatural illuminations, and heavenly visions; together with all the virtues and praises which are or shall be celebrated by all creatures in Heaven and on earth; for myself and all such as are recommended to my prayers; that by all Thou mayest be worthily praised and glorified forever.

4. Receive my wishes, O Lord, my God, and my desires of giving Thee infinite praise and immense blessings, which according to the multitude of Thine unspeakable greatness, are most justly due to Thee.

These I render, and desire to render Thee every day and every moment; and I invite and entreat all the heavenly spirits, and all the faithful, with my prayers and affections, to join with me in giving Thee praises and thanks.

5. Let all peoples, tribes, and tongues, praise Thee, and magnify Thy holy and sweet name, with the highest jubilation and ardent devotion. (Dan. 7:14).

And let all who reverently and devoutly celebrate Thy most high Sacrament, and receive it with full faith, find grace and mercy at Thy hands, and humbly pray for me, a sinful creature.

And when they shall have obtained their desired devotion and joyful union, and shall depart from Thy sacred heavenly table well comforted and wonderfully nourished, let them vouchsafe to remember my poor soul.

CHAPTER XVIII
That a Man Follow Christ

CHRIST

THOU must beware of curious and unprofitable searching into this most profound Sacrament, if thou wilt not sink into the depth of doubt.

"He that is a searcher of majesty shall be overwhelmed by glory." (Prov. 25:27). God is able to do more than man can understand.

A pious and humble inquiry after truth is tolerable, which is always ready to be taught, and studies to walk in the sound doctrine of the Fathers.

2. Blessed is that simplicity that leaveth the difficult ways of dispute, and goeth on in the plain and sure path of God's commandments. (Ps. 118:35).

Many have lost devotion whilst they would search into high things.

Faith is required of thee, and a sincere life, not the height of understanding, nor diving deep into the mysteries of God.

If thou dost not understand nor comprehend those things that are under thee, how shouldst thou comprehend those things that are above thee?

Submit thyself to God, and humble thy senses to faith, and the light of knowledge shall be given thee, as far as shall be profitable and necessary for thee.

3. Some are grievously tempted about faith and the Sacrament; but this is not to be imputed to them, but rather to the enemy.

Be not thou anxious, stand not to dispute with thy thoughts, nor to answer the doubts which the devil suggests; but believe the words of God, believe His saints and prophets, and the wicked enemy will fly from thee. (James 4:7).

It is often very profitable to the servants of God to suffer such things.

For the devil tempts not unbelievers and sinners, whom he already surely possesses; but the faithful and devout he many ways tempts and molests.

4. Go forward, therefore, with a sincere and undoubting faith, and with an humble reverence approach this Sacrament: and whatsoever thou art not able to understand commit securely to Almighty God.

God deceiveth thee not; but he is deceived that trusteth too much in himself.

God walketh with the simple, and revealeth Himself to the humble; He giveth understanding to the little ones, openeth the gate of knowledge to pure minds, and hideth His grace from the curious and proud. (Ps. 98:130; Matt. 11:25).

Human reason is weak, and may be deceived, but true faith cannot be deceived.

5. All reason and natural search ought to follow faith, and not to go before it, nor oppose it.

For faith and love are here predominant, and work by hidden ways in this most holy and superexcellent Sacrament.

God, who is eternal and incomprehensible, and of infinite power, doth great and inscrutable things in Heaven and earth, and there is no searching out His wonderful works. (Is. 40:28).

If the works of God were such as might be easily comprehended by human reason, they could not be called wonderful or unspeakable.